COMBAT AIRCRAFT

162

Fw 190 *SCHLACHT* UNITS

SERIES EDITOR TONY HOLMES

162 COMBAT AIRCRAFT

Robert Forsyth

Fw 190 *SCHLACHT* UNITS

OSPREY
PUBLISHING

OSPREY PUBLISHING
Bloomsbury Publishing Plc
Kemp House, Chawley Park, Cumnor Hill, Oxford, OX2 9PH, UK
Bloomsbury Publishing Ireland Limited,
29 Earlsfort Terrace, Dublin 2, D02 AY28, Ireland
1359 Broadway, 5th Floor, New York, NY 10018, USA
E-mail; info@ospreypublishing.com
www.ospreypublishing.com

OSPREY is a trademark of Osprey Publishing Ltd

First published in Great Britain in 2026

A catalogue record for this book is available from the British Library.

ISBN: PB 9781472867834; eBook 9781472867841; ePDF 9781472867858; XML 9781472867827

26 27 28 29 30 10 9 8 7 6 5 4 3 2 1

Edited by Tony Holmes
Cover Artwork by Gareth Hector
Aircraft Profiles by Janusz Światłoń
Index by Angela Hall
Typeset by Lumina Datamatics Ltd
Printed by Repro India Ltd

Osprey Publishing supports the Woodland Trust, the UK's leading woodland conservation charity.

To find out more about our authors and books visit **www.ospreypublishing.com**. Here you will find extracts, author interviews, details of forthcoming events and the option to sign up for our newsletter.

For product safety related questions contact productsafety@bloomsbury.com

Acknowledgements

My thanks to the following individuals for their kind assistance – Eddie Nielinger, Nick Beale, Martin Pegg, Dietmar Hermann, Tomáš Poruba, Daniel Horvath, Mick Oakey, Dr Richard P Hallion, Jay P Spenser, Marcel van Heijkop, Morten Jessen and Alexander Steenbeck. I am also grateful to the late Hermann Buchner.

Front Cover

Over a snow-covered landscape, a *Rotte* (section of two aircraft) of Fw 190F-8s from II./SG 2 in crude winter camouflage carry out a low-level bombing attack against a Soviet Army tank and vehicle column in western Hungary in January 1945 during operations in support of the attempted German relief of Budapest. At this time, II. *Gruppe*, under Major Götz Baumann, was deployed along with the *Geschwader's* other Fw 190-equipped *Gruppen* around Lake Balaton, engaged in intensive sorties against the Soviet drive towards Austria.

The Fw 190s depicted in this artwork are dropping AB 250 weapons containers on their target. The AB 250 would hold loads of two-, four- or ten-kilogramme *Splitterbomben* (fragmentation bombs), and was usually intended for use against 'soft-skinned' vehicles, but by this stage of the war ordnance depended on availability.

By January 1945, the bulk of the Fw 190 *Schlachtgruppen* were deployed in the east, fighting a dogged but outnumbered battle against the overwhelming armour and manpower of the Red Army (*Cover artwork by Gareth Hector*)

Previous Pages

An Fw 190F-8/R1 believed to be from *Stab* I./SG 77 at Seifersdorf in August 1944. As an R1, it is fitted with electrically operated underwing ETC 50 racks carrying four SC 50 bombs, as well as an SC 250 suspended from the fuselage. Also clearly visible here are the barrels of the two wing-mounted 20 mm MG 151/20 cannon (*EN Archive*)

CONTENTS

CHAPTER ONE

SCHLACHT

Schlacht is the German word for 'battle'. As in English, it can be coupled with another to create a more specific term. For example, in German, a battleship is a *Schlachtschiff*. Similarly, it was and remains a term used in the realm of air power. In 1943, one of a series of books was published intended as an aide for translators and linguists. Entitled *Luftfahrt-English – Flugzeugbau, Motorenkunde, Luftwaffe* (*Aeronautical English – Aircraft Construction, Engine Technology, Air Force*), in its section on definitions of aeronautical terms, the book explains a *'Schlachtflugzeug'* as being an 'Assault aircraft – Attack machines are used for making low flying attacks against ground targets'.

This description is entirely accurate, and at the time of the book's publication in 1943, Luftwaffe *Schlachtverbände* were indeed flying low-level missions with effect against ground targets over the USSR, North Africa and, eventually, southern Italy.

However, as a military/air power concept, the origins of the *Schlachtflugzeuge* stretched back before World War 1, when, in 1913, Major Wilhelm Siegert, an innovative officer and pilot serving in the embryonic German *Fliegertruppe*, envisaged aircraft being deployed over the battlefield as bombers and ground strafers, although at that time the weight of bombs and early machine guns were too heavy for the light and flimsy Rumpler, Albatros, Aviatik, Euler and LVG airframes then in use. Nevertheless, Siegert's ideas were recognised and studied.

The concept of using *Schlachtflugzeuge* ('Battle Aircraft'), such as these Halberstadt CL.II of *Schlachtstaffel* 27, was employed by the German *Fliegertruppe* during World War 1 to provide 'close support' on the battlefield in terms of infantry cooperation and artillery observation. Here, armourers load up wooden racks of stick grenades for fitment to the fuselage sides of the Halberstadts ahead of a sortie over the Western Front (*Robert Forsyth Collection*)

Then, in the ensuing war, on 21 August 1917, during bitter fighting in the Verdun sector, a new *Schlachtgeschwader* (ground-attack wing), whose prime roles were infantry cooperation and artillery observation, was deployed to support a counterattack. By the time the aircraft had finished their operations, they had expended 575 kg of bombs and 7600 rounds of ammunition against French positions. Although the German divisions in the area were not able to hold their line, their air power had successfully displayed direct and organised intervention in the ground *Schlacht*, providing 'close support' for the ground forces.

In the late autumn of 1917, a meeting took place of senior pilots from the *Schutzstaffeln* (*Schusta*), which had provided protection for army cooperation two-seaters and reconnaissance squadrons, and which had previously been instructed to attack enemy troops 'when not employed on the protection of artillery aeroplanes'. The question of whether a light and fast aircraft or a heavy, armoured type should be introduced for ground-attack and close air support work was settled in favour of light machines such as the Halberstadt CL IV and/or Hannover CL V biplanes. The observer would use a two-centimetre cannon to fire at targets on the battlefield or drop one-kilogramme fragmentation bombs known as *'Fliegermause'* ('flying mice').

Close air support techniques were again deployed in November 1917 near Passchendaele when Canadian ground forces reported being harassed by German formations comprised of three to nine aircraft at a time, appearing to operate using well-developed tactics.

Techniques were refined further so that by the beginning of the German offensive on the Somme in March 1918, 38 existing *Schusta* were officially reformed and redesignated as *Schlachtstaffeln* (*Schlasta*). The *Schusta* had become increasingly involved in ground-attack missions and localised offensive work from the summer of 1917, and such activity led organically, as mentioned, to the creation of the prototype *Schlachtgeschwader*. Indeed, by November 1917 ground-attack was the prime role of the *Schusta*.

During the Battle of Cambrai on 30 November, the Germans deployed every available *Schusta* in support of a counter-attack, with CL category machines – single-engined, armed, two-seat Halberstadt or Hannover biplanes – flying below 100 ft according to British reports. The British Army suffered heavy casualties under the weight of fire from German aircraft targeting frontline trenches and rear positions, and troops found the effect 'very demoralising'.

On 20 February 1918, Generalleutnant Ernst von Hoeppner, the *Kommandierender General der Luftstreitkräfte* (*Kogenluft* – Commanding General of the Air Service), issued official instructions that the *Schlasta* were to be 'employed at the decisive point of the attack' rather than being used singly, and therefore with less effect, over the whole length of front attack. Importantly, it was noted that 'the object of the *Schlasta* is to shatter the enemy's nerve by repeated attacks in close formation', and this was to be done in conjunction with an infantry assault.

The *Schlasta* were dispersed among corps headquarters or grouped into non-permanent *Schlachtgruppen*. During operations against the British sector on the Somme, the *Schlasta* gave support to German ground forces thrusting towards Amiens by attacking enemy positions in waves, in loose formation, at low level, using machine guns and dropping hand grenades.

Such was their effectiveness over the battlefield in a short time and their positive contribution to morale amongst the ground troops that it was proposed to increase the number of *Schlacht* units from 38 *Staffeln* to 60, forming six new *Schlachtgeschwader* each of six *Staffeln*.

In April 1918 four permanent *Schlachtgeschwader* were created, each with at least four *Staffeln*. The units would be based on airfields close to corps or divisional headquarters, where they could be kept in telephone contact with ground commanders. They would fly ahead of their own infantry with the intention of suppressing enemy infantry sheltering in their trenches or shell craters. Later, artillery batteries, ammunition dumps, supply columns and vehicles became targets. The lower an attack could be flown – ideally around 30–50 m – the more effective it was.

However, there was a problem that always dogged such operations. The reality was that the *Schlachtflieger* were only able to deliver offensive loads of up to 12 infantry stick grenades, and it was not until June 1918 that crews finally started carrying five two-kilogramme anti-personnel bombs. That month von Hoeppner wrote to General of the Infantry General Erich Ludendorff, 'Physical and moral success can be achieved only through heavy attacks by massed *Schlachtfliegern*'. But by then the armistice was less than six months away.

ACTION IN SPAIN

Eighteen years later, in September 1936, at the commencement of Nazi Germany's intervention in the Spanish Civil War, two dismantled examples of the Henschel Hs 123 biplane arrived by ship at Cadiz. Moved on to Tablada airfield for reassembly, the Luftwaffe hoped that these aircraft could be assessed for their potential as dive-bombers within an operational environment. The aircraft were assigned to *Versuchsjagdstaffel* (experimental fighter squadron) 88, established by the *Legion Condor*, the Luftwaffe's operational command in Spain. The type debuted in combat as a dive-bomber over the Malaga front in January 1937.

The Luftwaffe's *Legion Condor* trialled the use of adapted *Schlachtflugzeuge* during the Spanish Civil War. Although results were initially mixed, the *Legion*'s efforts provided RLM planners with valuable insight into tactics and aircraft effectiveness. Here, armourers fuse ten-kilogramme bombs ready for use on a Heinkel He 45 reconnaissance machine of A/88 – one such type that was occasionally used in the *Schlacht* role, with ordnance carried either in a bay behind the observer or on underwing racks (*Robert Forsyth Collection*)

A handful of Henschel biplanes, known as *Angelitos*, subsequently carried out sporadic low-level bombing and dive-bombing sorties against Republican targets. On 14 March, while on a bombing and reconnaissance mission, the Hs 123s strafed personnel at a railway crossing between Villanueva and Alcaracejos in what may have been a very brief, but early example of deliberate 'ground-attack' as distinct from bombing. On 27 March, four Hs 123s carried out a low-level attack against the Palace of Zarzuela and nearby Republican trenches, although one aircraft was shot down.

The Henschels were not alone. In reality, other single-engined aircraft to reach Spain – the Heinkel He 51 biplane and the advanced Messerschmitt Bf 109 fighter, as well as the Junkers Ju 87 dive-bomber – all carried out free-range strafing and bombing attacks over battle areas.

Although the Hs 123 was seen by Generalluftzeugmeister Ernst Udet and others in the *Reichsluftministerium* (RLM) as a dive-bomber, the Chief of Staff of the *Legion Condor*, Oberst Wolfram *Freiherr* von Richthofen, was of the opinion that the type could equally be deployed as a *Schlachtflugzeug*. However, the biplane lacked any radio equipment for ground and air communications, and signalling methods used in-theatre were primitive. Von Richthofen further believed that an aircraft in a dive would always be susceptible to anti-aircraft (AA) fire while 'locked' in approaching its dive, hence a preference for shallow, low-level attacks on ground targets.

In Spain, the *Legion Condor* was able to carry out honest assessments of its aircraft in operational conditions, and when it came to *Schlacht* (close air support and pure ground-attack, not dive-bombing), existing doctrine dictated that such operations should be employed only in conditions of air superiority and used at decisive points with as much strength as possible.

Like the Hs 123, the He 51 had arrived in Spain in 1936. An elegant biplane and an effective fighter for its generation, it was nevertheless troublesome to maintain and had an outdated engine. In addition to its standard fighter role, the Heinkel would often, as described, carry out *Schlacht* sorties when possible. During operations at Brunete, He 51s would fly below 150 m in formations of nine aircraft abreast, strafing with machine guns and bombing Republican troops and AA batteries with their individual loads of six ten-kilogramme fragmentation bombs, dropping them simultaneously.

Senior Republican officers on the Madrid Front described how such machine gun fire kept their troops pinned to the ground, preventing them from using their weapons and causing panic and confusion in the rear areas. By the time the Heinkels had completed their runs, the attacking Nationalist troops were within hand grenade range of the Republicans. The commander of the 18th Army Corps felt the *Schlacht* attacks to be a 'disaster' for Republican forces, paralysing their defensive efforts. Oberleutnant Harro Harder, commander of the *Legion Condor* fighter unit 1. J/88, recalled one such mission;

'We were greeted by a real display of fireworks. Shells burst beside, above and below us, sometimes almost right in our machines. We went over to a low-level attack and were met by intense 20 mm fire from every direction.

Everywhere one looked there were He 51s dancing and attacking through the AA fire. The battle lasted about eight minutes, until we had dropped all of our bombs. Although we had almost no ammunition or bombs left, we so shook the Red infantry that they left their positions and ran in headlong flight.'

Making his combat debut at Brunete was Leutnant Adolf Galland, who would go on to enjoy a meteoric rise in the wartime Luftwaffe fighter force, eventually becoming its commanding general. He recalled flying *Schlacht* sorties in Spain in the He 51;

'We flew in close formation very low up the valleys, approaching the enemy position from the rear. At a signal [from the formation leader], the bombs were simultaneously released, and our load went down in a cluster. We called this "the little man's bomb-carpet".'

The He 51 biplane fighter was used by the *Legion Condor's* J/88 to conduct low-level strafing and bombing runs against Republican positions in a crude, but effective demonstration of *Schlacht* tactics in the Spanish Civil War (*Robert Forsyth Collection*)

NEW UNITS

As the war in Spain raged, and following the annexation of Austria, the *Führer*, Adolf Hitler, turned his attention to the Sudetenland, the western border of Czechoslovakia. As geopolitical tensions increased, between February and May 1938, five new *Schlachtfliegergruppen* (SFG) were hurriedly raised to be ready for intervention, and in doing so the '*Schlacht*' designation as used during World War 1 was once more adopted. Operationally, the Wehrmacht saw the targets for such units as including enemy infantry in deployment, or dug-in, or similarly dispersed targets. However, since such targets could, practicably, only be located, identified and attacked by low-level flights, these tasks would be assigned to the *Schlachtgruppen*.

SFGs 10 and 20 commenced training at Tutow in August, SFGs 30 and 40 at Fassberg at around the same time, and SFG 50 was also established at Lechfeld. In reality, these were hotchpotch formations scraped together by drawing on personnel from training schools, as well as small cadres of more experienced airmen who were provided with a mix of Focke-Wulf and Heinkel biplane trainers and a few examples of the more substantial He 51. As soon as was possible, their trainers were to be replaced by Hs 123s, but this took place across the units with differing effect.

The *Schlachtfliegergruppen* were always viewed as a measure of expedience, and by the autumn, with the conclusion of the Sudeten problem in October, they had largely been dissolved. One experienced *Schlachtflieger* officer told Allied interrogators after the war that the dominance of the Ju 87 dive-bomber in German doctrinal thinking 'amounted to a reverse suffered by the protagonists of real close [air] support, which was a term held to mean more or less direct and continuous participation in the land battle'.

Elements from the short-lived *Schlachtfliegergruppen*, however, were used to form Hs 123-equipped II.(*Schlacht*) *Gruppe* of *Lehrgeschwader* (LG) 2 at Tutow in November 1938. The *Gruppe* was assigned to von Richthofen's *Fliegerführer zbV*, a specialist bombing, dive-bombing and ground-attack command mainly flying Ju 87s, for the campaign against Poland where, with 40 Henschels on strength, it carried out the first ground-attack mission of the war on 1 September 1939. II.(*Schlacht*)/LG 2 was the only such unit in the Luftwaffe at the time.

This state of affairs was at least in part attributable to the belief of Generalmajor Hans Jeschonnek, the Luftwaffe Chief of General Staff, that *Schlacht* operations were a generally dangerous undertaking with potential for high attrition, especially in a situation where the enemy enjoyed even local air superiority. As such, Jeschonnek ordered that *Schlacht* missions should be conducted only where the results would comfortably achieve success. This meant that there was, metaphorically, a line in the sand between the notion of the Luftwaffe providing 'aerial artillery' in the way Ju 87 dive-bombers could, and the direct close air support for ground forces provided by the *Schlacht* units.

In Poland, II.(*Schlacht*)/LG 2 operated from four airfields in 21 days. The sortie rates were intensive – on occasion, Hs 123 pilots would fly up to ten missions per day. In his post-war study of the Luftwaffe in Poland, *General der Flieger* Wilhelm Speidel wrote that, 'Immediately after a dive-bomber attack, ground-attack aircraft took off in low-level attacks against the still paralysed enemy defences. In other cases, the ground-attack aircraft supported the ground forces directly, searching out their own targets within the battle area. Finally, they would make a surprise appearance at low altitudes in the enemy rear, where they would attack movements on roads'.

Despite the overall swiftness and military success of the German campaign in Poland, lessons were learned in terms of the nascent *Schlachtflieger* tactics. A report prepared by the Operations Officer of II.(*Schlacht*)/LG 2 immediately after the conclusion of the campaign contradicted Speidel's account and revealed that the tactics of low approach and low-level attack were, apparently, abandoned in Poland. The reasons cited were the great difficulties in finding targets, the danger from enemy ground fire and from bomb blast and shrapnel, the great physical and mental strain on pilots and the very great difficulty in distinguishing friendly and enemy forces.

An Hs 123 biplane of 6.(*Schlacht*)/LG 2 parked in its wooded dispersal in the West in the spring of 1940. This capable and rugged, but often overlooked, aeroplane saw service with the Luftwaffe in the ground-attack and infantry support roles from the Spanish Civil War to the Eastern Front in 1944. Note the SC 50 50-kg bombs and ammunition crates lying on the ground beneath the port wing (*EN Archive*)

Rather, the most commonly used tactic employed by the *Schlachtflieger* was to attack from the battle line with two or three *Schwärme* (four-aircraft formations), approaching at an altitude of between 800 to 2000 m, breaking off at 200 to 800 m. Ideally, attacks were made from various directions, and after completion, the Henschels would pull up and make a new attack.

'There is no doubt that this method of attack brings the greatest practical and moral success', the report stated, 'as the decisive effects at Czestochowa and on the Bzura have shown'.

One area that needed rectifying, however, was the poor installation of the Hs 123's two fuselage-mounted 7.92 mm MG 17 machine guns and their ammunition. When fired, damage was frequently sustained by the propeller, and the guns jammed regularly. This resulted in an increased need for new parts.

In terms of operations, it was more of the same in May 1940, when, during the German attack in Belgium and France, Hs 123s of II.(*Schlacht*)/LG 2, this time operating under VIII. *Fliegerkorps* control (von Richthofen's new command), rendered close support to XIX. *Panzerkorps* as it struck across the Meuse. Operations were also conducted successfully against concentrations of enemy troops around Sedan, Liège and Namur. With around 30 Henschels, the *Gruppe* earned gratitude from the Wehrmacht on 22 May when it accounted for the destruction of some 40 French tanks that were massing north of Cambrai in readiness for an attack.

Despite the *Schlacht* units' effectiveness in localised operations in Poland and France, they were greatly outnumbered by Ju 87 dive-bomber units. The Stuka was able to carry a larger bombload, and in Poland and the West the *Sturzkampfgeschwader* had proved very successful in dive-bombing specific targets in enemy forward and rear positions. The dive-bomber had won the minds of the decision-makers within the RLM.

As early as 21 September 1940, a detailed and lengthy report on the conduct of operations by units of VIII. *Fliegerkorps* in support of the Wehrmacht prepared by Oberstleutnant Wilhelm Deichmann, Adjutant to Generalmajor von Richthofen, failed to even mention the Hs 123 or the *Schlacht* units. The focus, understandably at this time, was on the Ju 87 and the Bf 109, the latter adapted as a fighter-bomber. However, this mindset would be challenged when Hitler and his generals turned their eyes eastwards towards their next ambition, the USSR, and a campaign which would demand the service of another superlative aircraft for the *Schlacht* role in an altogether more hostile environment. Enter the Focke-Wulf Fw 190.

The crew of a Ju 87B-1 of the *Stab* II./StG 2 pose with a member of their groundcrew at what is believed to be in the spring of 1940. Undoubtedly an effective aircraft, feared by its enemies in the early years of the war, the Ju 87 tended to be over-favoured in RLM doctrine, which frequently blurred the line between dive-bombing and close air support. From late 1943 onwards, with improvements in Allied and Soviet fighters and AA guns, and in their numbers, the Stuka became increasingly vulnerable (*EN Archive*)

Arado-built Fw 190F-8 Wk-Nr 582075 at Königsberg-Neumark in the summer of 1944 (*EN Archive*)

CHAPTER TWO

GROUND-ATTACK Fw 190

For the first 18 months of Operation *Barbarossa* – the German invasion of the Soviet Union commencing in June 1941 – Luftwaffe close-support and ground-attack missions were carried out principally by Ju 87 dive-bomber units and II.(*Schlacht*)/LG 2. In addition to its Hs 123s, since the summer of 1940, the latter *Gruppe* had been equipped with Bf 109E-7 fighter-bombers. Assigned again to VIII. *Fliegerkorps*, the *Gruppe* supported *Panzergruppe* 3 in the northern sector of Army Group Centre as it advanced from Suwalki towards Grodno.

By July, II.(*Schlacht*)/LG 2 was covering the heavy fighting around Smolensk, and from then until the end of the year it maintained an intense level of operations, December seeing the *Gruppe* supporting the German advance towards Moscow and the fighting south of Lake Ilmen. The Bf 109E-7 was a development of the E-4 variant of the Luftwaffe's standard single-engined fighter, featuring an improved oil system to counter the effect on engine lubrication caused by drag as a result of the fitment of bomb racks and bombs. This enhancement allowed the E-7 to carry 50-kg, 500-kg or SD-2 fragmentation bombs or, alternatively, a 300-litre drop tank to extend its range.

In August 1940, II.(*Schlacht*)/LG 2 was one of the first units to take on the Bf 109E-7, and a number of fighter *Gruppen* followed so that by the end of 1941, a handful of *Jagdgeschwadern* (JG) including JGs 2, 26, 27 and 52 were using the variant in the *'Jabo'* (*Jagd-Bomber* – fighter-bomber) role.

In the autumn of 1942, the new radial-engined Fw 190 fighter made its debut over the Eastern Front after I./JG 51 had converted to the type from the Bf 109. It was followed, for a period, by III. *Gruppe* and then elements of JG 54. The Fw 190 soon proved suitable for the operating environment of the Eastern Front, offering greater armament 'punching power' than the Bf 109, which, for example, had had to be retro-fitted with underwing 20 mm cannon gondolas in order to bring down heavily armoured Soviet Ilyushin Il-2 ground-attack aircraft. Such installations had a negative impact on the Messerschmitt's manoeuvrability. Furthermore, the radiator on the Bf 109's liquid-cooled Daimler-Benz DB 601 engine was vulnerable to the rearward defensive fire from an Il-2.

By comparison, the Fw 190 fielded four 20 mm cannon comfortably with no adverse effect on manoeuvrability, and although the Bf 109 could turn a little quicker, the Focke-Wulf was faster in a half-roll. The fighter's big BMW 801 radial engine offered protection for its pilot and, importantly for ground-attack deployment, its air-cooled system was relatively less susceptible to damage from ground fire. Also, its wide-tracked undercarriage was good for rudimentary frontline airstrips.

By the spring of 1943, a small number of Fw 190A-4 fighters, and their pilots, of I./JG 54 had been redesignated a '*Jaboschwarm*' under the command of the *Gruppenadjutant*, Oberleutnant Edwin Dutel, who became known as the '*Jabo* King'. The *Schwarm* would carry out low-level ground-strafing runs against Soviet troops or strike at targets on the 'ice road' across the frozen Lake Ladoga, dropping either 'oil bombs' loaded with high-explosive and petrol, heavy demolition bombs or two-kilogramme SD 2 'butterfly' anti-personnel bombs – nasty weapons which were painted white so that they could not be easily detected against the snow. Dutel was lost on 9 April while carrying out a low-level mission southeast of Schlüsselburg and east of Leningrad.

Equipped with Fw 190A-5s, most of 4./JG 54 was functioning in the *Jabo* role and operating under IV. *Gruppe* in the northern sector of the frontline by the summer. The *Staffel* even went so far as to adopt letter fuselage codes rather than the customary fighter-style numerals, replicating the style used by the *Schlachtstaffeln*.

Similarly, on 15 January 1943 at Petsamo in the far north, elements of 11./JG 5 were redesignated 14.(*Jabo*)/JG 5 and equipped with the Fw 190A-3. The *Staffel* existed for only 12 months, but in that time it conducted attacks on enemy shipping, accounting for significant tonnage damaged or sunk, as well as against Soviet airfields and transport. Such was the *Staffel's* success that its *Kapitän*, Hauptmann Friedrich-Wilhelm Strakeljahn, was awarded the Knight's Cross. But, strictly speaking, these were *fighter-bomber* missions performed by *fighters*, and it is important to make the distinction between such operations and those of the *Schlachtgruppen*.

The modus operandi of the *Schlacht* units was to strike at targets on the battlefield, or close to it, and to eliminate resistance locally for ground forces through close air support. *Jabos* were free to attack targets at far greater range behind enemy lines – either on a pre-determined basis or often as 'harassers', or against shipping, bridges and railways, as well as, on occasion, close-support targets. Historically, the waters have been muddied by various generalised terms such as 'fighter-bomber' (*Jabo*), 'light bomber', 'fast-bomber' (*Schnellbomber*), '*Blitzbomber*', battle aircraft (*Kampfflugzeug*) and ground-attack/close-support aircraft (*Schlachtflugzeug*). In a post-war study prepared for the USAF, former Luftwaffe senior officer *General der Flieger* Josef Kammhuber contended the following definitions;

- A fighter aircraft is a military aeroplane designed for offensive action *in* the air
- A bomber aircraft is a military aeroplane designed for offensive action *from* the air
- A fighter-bomber is a military aeroplane designed for offensive action both *in* and *from* the air, the greater emphasis being on action *from* the air.

In accordance with Kammhuber's definitions, a *Schlachtflugzeug* should be categorised as a bomber, but that is misleading. Equally, unlike a *Jabo*, a *Schlachtflugzeug* was not intended to operate as a fighter, nor were *Schlacht* pilots trained as fighter pilots. The *Schlachtflugzeuge* and the *Schlachtflieger* were *ground-attack/close-support* specialists intended to operate directly over the battlefield or at 'decisive' points related to it.

A major step in the expansion of the *Schlachtflieger* occurred in January 1942 with the establishment of *Schlachtgeschwader* (Schl.G.) 1 at Werl, near Dortmund, under the command of Major Otto Weiss, the same officer who, as *Gruppenkommandeur* of II.(*Schlacht*)/LG 2, led the successful *Schlacht* actions in France in 1940. Weiss had been awarded the Knight's Cross on 18 May 1940, followed by the Oak Leaves on 31 December 1941.

To help form Schl.G. 1, Weiss was assisted by most of his former staff from II.(*Schlacht*)/LG 2 – all experienced *Schlacht* officers. Upon formation, the *Geschwader* comprised two *Gruppen* – I./Schl.G. 1, equipped initially with Bf 109E-7s, and II. *Gruppe* equipped with Hs 123s and the new Hs 129 twin-engined anti-tank aircraft. Two semi-independent anti-tank *Staffeln*, 4.(Pz) and 8.(Pz)/Schl.G. 1, were also formed in the USSR equipped initially with Bf 109s before converting to the Hs 129.

Concurrent to the re-equipping of JGs 51 and 54, I./Schl.G. 1 converted to the Fw 190A-5 in April 1943, its aircraft arriving as U3 sub-variants, together with a small number of U8s. By this time, the *Gruppe* was under the acting command of Hauptmann Georg Dörffel. He had joined Schl.G. 1 at its formation, becoming *Kapitän* of 5. *Staffel*. Initially trained as a bomber observer, he had volunteered for the *Schlachtflieger* in the late 1930s. While in France in May 1940, like Otto Weiss, Dörffel had demonstrated his aptitude flying the Hs 123 to strike at French tanks in the Cambrai area. He went on to become a highly successful ground-attack airman, and in April 1943, at around the time he took command of I./Schl.G. 1, Dörffel was awarded the Oak Leaves to the Knight's Cross.

Between October 1942 and March 1943, the *Gruppe* had been involved in strenuous air operations in the southern sector of the Eastern Front, including close air support missions around Stalingrad and in the attempt to hold back the Red Army thrust through the Donets Basin. During the latter operation the unit lost several pilots and aircraft to enemy ground-fire, fighters and terrible weather.

As mentioned, to replace its Bf 109s, I./Schl.G. 1 received the Fw 190A-5. Somewhat surprisingly, the development of the fighter had often been protracted and tortuous. Following a specification issued to Focke-Wulf Flugzeugbau GmbH by the RLM in 1937 for an aircraft with a performance which would be superior to that of the, at the time, new and largely untested Bf 109, Dipl.-Ing. Kurt Tank, the firm's Technical Director, and his design team at Bremen dutifully turned to the drawing board.

Focke-Wulf saw a rugged aircraft built first and foremost for interception, and therefore able to absorb considerable punishment in action, and not specifically for attack missions – a tack which did not find favour with the prevailing German air doctrine which envisioned a short, offensive war. However, Tank, a resolute and exceptionally gifted designer, remained undaunted. He believed that an air-cooled radial engine was capable of withstanding more combat stress than the liquid-cooled, inline Daimler-Benz favoured by Messerschmitt. Because his design would not, therefore, impinge upon production of the Bf 109's DB 601, the RLM eventually relented and permitted Focke-Wulf to proceed.

Focke-Wulf took time and considerable effort to ensure that structure and build were second to none, and that the design would demand the minimum of maintenance in operating conditions. The company was fortunate in that no less a figure than Reichsmarschall Hermann Göring viewed the new aircraft with enthusiasm.

In February 1941, six pre-production Fw 190A-0s were delivered to the test unit *Erprobungsstaffel* 190. Despite some difficulties associated with the propeller mechanism, and overheating and compressor damage to the BMW 801 engines, by August 1941 things were deemed safe enough to allow the first Fw 190A-1 production machines, each armed with four

A pair of SC 50 bombs have been fitted to the twin underwing ETC 50 racks on this Fw 190A-5, KD+MD (*EN Archive*)

7.92 mm MG 17 machine guns and two 20 mm Oerlikon MG FF cannon in the outer wings, to be handed over to 6./JG 26 in Belgium, where they replaced the *Staffel's* Bf 109Es.

Towards the end of the year, deliveries of the Fw 190A-2 to JG 26 commenced, this variant featuring an improved 1600 hp BMW 801C2 and an uprated weapons array which included two 20 mm Mauser MG 151 cannon built into the wing roots, with interrupter gear incorporated to allow synchronised fire through the propeller arc.

JG 26 received the A-3 fitted with the new 1700 hp BMW 801D-2 engine in April 1942, the uprated power achieved by increasing the compression ratio in the cylinders and refinements to the two-speed supercharger. Externally, the variant was equipped with a pair of MG 17s and a pair of MG 151/20s. Production continued into 1943, reaching a total of 509 machines built. The A-3 was also graced with the ability to adapt easily to the role of a *Jabo* using a series of *Umbau* (factory modifications), as the A-3/U1 (by means of installation of an ETC 500 bomb rack), the U3 (ETC 250 fuselage rack and SC 50 underwing racks) and the U7 sub-variants.

The Fw 190A-4 was developed into a fully 'convertible fighter/fighter-bomber', with low-level capability provided by an MW 50 power boost system when flying below 5000 m. Capitalising on the A-3's adaptability, the Fw 190A-4, although carrying the same fixed armament as its predecessor, introduced an even more wide-ranging and sophisticated family of sub-variants. The A-4/U1, with only two MG 151s for armament, was fitted with two ETC 501 bomb racks for carrying a pair of SC 250 bombs, while the A-4/U3 emerged in October 1942 as a true 'assault' aircraft, being fitted with a six-millimetre armour ring ahead of the cowling and five-millimetre steel armour plates beneath the cowling and cockpit designed to protect the pilot, fuel tanks and

With its BMW 801D-2 engine idling, this Fw 190F-2, has been fitted with a centreline ETC 501 bomb rack from which is suspended a 500-kg SC 500 bomb. With such a load, the aircraft's speed was compromised by some 100 km/h (*EN Archive*)

engine on ground-attack missions. The A-4/U8 was a long-range fighter-bomber, fitted with a 300-litre drop tank and four SC 50 bombs on wing racks, together with full armament. Benefiting from MW 50, the A-4 also carried a FuG 16Z VHF transceiver.

From April 1943, the Fw 190A-4 was superseded by the A-5. With the exception of a lengthened fuselage (by 15 cm) and strengthened housing for its BMW 801D-2 engine, the A-5, of which 723 were built up to the summer of 1943, was essentially unaltered from the A-4, but offered an even more inventive selection of sub-variants, reflecting the versatility of the Focke-Wulf fighter. Provision was made for cannon, drop tanks and fuselage and wing-mounted bombs, as well as 21 cm underwing air-to-air mortars for operations against formations of American bombers. Those Fw 190A-5s delivered to I./Schl.G. 1 were configured as U3s, fitted with ETC 501 under-fuselage racks able to carry a maximum load of 1000 kg, although armament was restricted to fuselage-mounted MG 17s.

Meanwhile, in an effort to avoid cumbersome suffixes and, because of increasing operational demands, it was decided to delineate *Schlacht* machines from fighters by creating a new 'F' production series. This commenced with the Fw 190F-1, which was, in reality, an Fw 190A-4/U3 completed with its U3 *Umbau* fully incorporated and without MG FF cannon. However, unlike the Fw 190A-4/U3, the F-1 *Schlachtflugzeug* could not (easily) be 'retro-converted' to fighter configuration. It is believed some 25–30 such machines were so delivered before production went over to the F-2.

Based on the Fw 190A-5/U3, the Fw 190A-6 was originally intended as a dedicated *Schlachtflugzeug*, but in fact the 'A-6' designation was assigned to the following fighter variant. Just over 270 examples of what emerged instead as the Fw 190F-2 were produced between December 1942 and May 1943, featuring increased armour as well as external intakes to which tropical filters could be fitted.

An Fw 190F-2 fitted with a supplementary ER 4 bomb rack attached to its ETC 501. This enabled the carriage of four 50-kg SC 50 bombs, but in flight tests it was found that the aircraft's speed was reduced by 96 km/h with such a load (*EN Archive*)

However, as 'merely' enhanced and/or adapted A variants, the F-1 and F-2 had restricted offensive under-fuselage load parameters. This meant that in carrying only a single 250- or 500-kg bomb, if the weapon failed after release, there was no further bomb with which to conduct a second attack run. Thus, the ensuing Fw 190F-3 became a hybrid, created by fitting the stronger wing of the A-6 fighter to the A-5 fuselage, thus allowing a greater payload. Armament comprised two MG 17s and two 20 mm MG 151 cannon.

The F-4 to F-7 variants remained at the planning or developmental stage only, but commencing March 1944, the F-8, based on the armoured Fw 190A-8 '*Sturm*' fighter used in the defence of the Reich in 1944, featured a BMW 801D-2 engine, 13 mm MG 131 machine guns over the engine and MG 151 cannon in the wing roots. A FuG 16 ZS radio was installed, without Y-*Verfahren* (Y-directional equipment), but with a ZVG 16 homing unit.

From August 1944, the F-8 incorporated an extra fuel tank of 115 litres built in behind the cockpit that extended range but, as a result, required the ETC 501 rack to be lengthened by 200 mm and moved forward to offset the centre of gravity. As the F-8/U1 *Umbau*, additionally the aircraft could carry two underwing ETC 503 racks for SC 250 bombs or drop tanks. Further *Umbau* and *Rüstsatze* (conversion kits) allowed a myriad of (theoretical) load options and installations including aerial torpedoes, cannon, drop tanks and radio equipment.

Simultaneous in development to the F series was the G series of *Jagdbomber mit grosser Reichweite* (or '*Jabo-Rei*' – extended-range fighter-bombers), which was, in essence, a progression of those earlier bomb rack-fitted A series *Umbau* variants. The G-1 was, in reality, the A-4/U8 – a *Jabo* configured fighter able to carry a 300-litre fuselage-mounted drop tank as well as underwing bombs. The G-2 was almost identical, but had strengthened landing gear. Production of the Fw 190G-3 commenced from August 1943, incorporating a *Kuto Nase* barrage balloon cable-cutting device fitted to wing leading edges for nocturnal fighter-bomber missions. This variant could achieve a range of 1536 km at 427.2 km/h.

In a somewhat complex but logical policy, the ensuing G-4 became the G-8 in order that, in documents and planning, it could bȩ related with the A-8 fighter and F-8 *Schlacht* variants (the proposed G-5 and G-6 would become the G-9 and G-10 – there was no production of the G-7). The Fw 190G-8 *Jabo* was intended for longer-range work and, accordingly, was fitted with a FuG 16 ZY radio, GM-1 equipment and PKS 11 or PKS 12 directional control. To carry its offensive load, the aircraft had an ETC 501 rack beneath the fuselage for a bomb (or drop tank), and underwing ETC 503 racks could carry drop tanks. To offset the extra weight, armament was reduced to two MG 151s in the wing roots, and in line with the G-8's foreseen night missions, a proposal was also made to equip it with a Zeiss 130 E searchlight.

Like so many German military aircraft of World War 2, the Fw 190, while undoubtedly a superlative fighter, had been subjected to a series of adaptations, conversions and 'extras' in order to configure it as a ground-attack aircraft for deployment with the *Schlachtflieger*. From the spring of 1943, only time would tell how well placed the RLM's faith was.

CHAPTER THREE

SOVIET UNION – 1943

Groundcrew line up in front of an Fw 190A-5/U3 of 6./Schl.G 2 at Deblin-Irena in January 1943. The aircraft carries the unit's Mickey Mouse insignia and has a centreline ETC 501 bomb rack fitted. Note aircraft 'N' to the right. Both Fw 190s would have also carried the black triangle marking of the *Schlachtflieger* aft of their fuselage *Balkenkreuze* (*EN Archive*)

On 18 March 1943, away from the battlefields of the Soviet Union, the Commander in Chief of the Luftwaffe, Reichsmarschall Göring, chaired a production conference at Carinhall, his plush country residence in the Schorfheide Forest, northeast of Berlin. His view was that Germany's aircraft and aero-engineering industries had failed the nation, and he was bitter about it. He chided the assembled aircraft designers, engineers and RLM officials 'about the complete failure which has resulted in practically all fields of aeronautical engineering'. In Göring's eyes, even standard types such as the Bf 109 and Ju 88 were failing since many examples were being 'delivered in a half-finished condition and have to be completed when they reach the squadrons'.

However, he did at least concede that 'the Fw 190 could perhaps be considered as a very effective fighter-bomber', but even then he saw shortcomings in a revision of the type's fuel storage which, in his view, meant that 'the whole advantage has been lost'.

In mid-May, by the time *Stab* and I./Schl.G. 1 had completed their conversion to the Fw 190A-5, in the southern sector of the Eastern Front, German forces held a line from Belgorod in the north to the Sea of Azov in the south. It was almost stalemate, but May would prove to be a difficult month for the German leadership. On the 5th, bad news came from the Kuban, where Krymsk and Neberjaisk were retaken by the Red Army. Despite Generalfeldmarschall Erich von Manstein's victory at Kharkov at the conclusion of the 1942–43 winter campaign, the loss of Stalingrad in

February still reverberated painfully at all levels of German forces in the East, as well as the *Oberkommando des Heeres* (OKH – Army High Command).

Now Hitler vacillated over Operation *Zitadelle*, the planned armoured summer offensive aimed at sealing off the 150 km-wide by 65 km-deep Soviet thrust between Orel in the north and Belgorod in the south, centred on the city of Kursk. On 10 May, during a meeting between Hitler and his Inspector General of Armoured Forces, General Heinz Guderian, intended to explore ways of increasing tank production, Guderian questioned the rationale behind *Zitadelle*. 'Why do you want to attack in the East at all?' According to Guderian, Hitler was queasy about the whole venture. On 6 May, the OKH announced the postponement of the offensive until 12 June. A week later, on 13 May, the remaining Axis forces in Tunisia surrendered.

At this time Schl.G. 1 was under the command of Oberstleutnant Hubertus Hitschhold, a veteran Stuka pilot and former *Kommandeur* of I. *Stukageschwader* (StG) 2, a *Gruppe* he led throughout the campaign in the West and against Britain in 1940. Later flying over the Balkans and Crete, he was credited with sinking or damaging up to 164,000 tons of shipping in dive-bombing attacks. Hitschhold was decorated with the Oak Leaves to the Knight's Cross on 31 December 1941, while at the time serving as *Kommandeur* of the Stuka training school *Sturzkampffliegerschule* 1 at Wertheim.

Leading I./Schl.G. 1 was Hauptmann Georg Dörffel (see Chapter Two). In the meantime, II./Schl.G. 1, under Knight's Cross-holder Hauptmann Frank Neubert (although he had been shot down and wounded by Soviet AA fire on 30 January) and previously equipped with Hs 129s, Hs 123s and Bf 109Es, had, apart from 7. *Staffel*, also completed transition to the Fw 190 by the first week of March. The *Gruppe* then moved to Pavlograd, in Ukraine, for operational training, and by mid-April the unit was at its new base of Anapa on the Black Sea coast in the northern Caucasus. Here, the Focke-Wulfs and Henschels were engaged in carrying out intense ground-attack missions in support of the German 17. *Armee*.

Hauptmann Frank Neubert, seen here as an Oberleutnant after receiving the Knight's Cross, served as *Kommandeur* of II./Schl.G. 1. He flew most of the aircraft types used by the *Schlachtgruppen* in some 350 missions. In the latter half of the war, he commanded training units and worked with the Staff of the *General der Schlachtflieger* (*EN Archive*)

By early February 1943, 1. *Panzerarmee* had been pulled back in a long, hard retreat under bitterly cold temperatures and with the enemy chasing it all the way into the southern Ukraine to join *Heeresgruppe Don*. This left 17. *Armee* retreating towards the Taman Peninsula and isolated in the Kuban with some 350,000 men and 2000 artillery pieces. Instead of being bottled up there, with its back to the Sea of Azov, such a force could have been much better utilised in the main frontline. Hitler, however, decided that the *Armee*'s position on what was to become known as the Kuban bridgehead should be held, as it was considered to be in a strong spot from which to tie down large Soviet forces and to keep open a route to the Caucasus' oil fields.

The Soviet Air Force outnumbered the Luftwaffe over the Kuban by about four-to-one, while the Red Army's growing number of AA batteries were also gaining a fearsome reputation in this theatre. Between 10–17 May, II./Schl.G. 1 lost at least seven Fw 190A-5s while attacking targets in the Abinskaya and Krymskaya areas, most of them to ground fire. Conditions were made more uncomfortable by regular Soviet bombing raids on Anapa airfield.

Aside from the threat posed by the enemy, Schl.G. 1 was also faced with dissolution by the Luftwaffe. On 1 May, Generaloberst von Richthofen, the commander of *Luftflotte* 4 in southern Russia, noted that 'a strengthening of the *Schlachtfliegerverbände*, including [by] those which have been freed up in Africa, is out of the question'.

At the same time, the Luftwaffe Chief of General Staff, Generaloberst Hans Jeschonnek, informed von Richthofen that 'he had no objection to the dissolution of the *Geschwaderstab*', and was happy for *Luftflotte* 4 to take care of matters. Jeschonnek stressed that if this did indeed happen, Hitschhold was not to be left redundant, and that, ideally, he should be posted to one of the Stuka *Geschwader* as *Kommodore*. Despite these high-level discussions, Schl.G. 1 remained in existence for another five months, although Hitschhold would depart within weeks.

Both *Stab* and I. *Gruppe* moved to Barvenkovo in mid-May, with the *Stab* arriving from Voroshilovgrad and I. *Gruppe* from Kharkov-Nord. The Fw 190s quickly went into action, supporting ground forces in the heavy fighting around Izyum. On 22 May, IV. *Fliegerkorps* deployed the *Schlachtflieger* to good effect against enemy troop assemblies around Izyum and Priwolnoje, as well as against Red Army vehicles on roads around Tichorezk, Rostov–Swoboda, Poworino and airfields in the Orlowka–Morosowskaja–Possosch–Urasow area. At the end of the month, operating in conjunction with Stukas, Fw 190s again targeted Izyum and Priwolnoje.

II./Schl.G. 1 received a boost in June when it took delivery of the first Fw 190F-3s, which offered improved armour protection for the *Schlachtflieger*. On 1 July, the unit reported 15 Fw 190A-5s, 18 Fw 190F-3s and 16 Hs 123Bs on strength.

On 3 June, together with Ju 87s, *Schlacht* Fw 190s attacked the enemy airfield known to the Germans as Starobjelsk II, as well as the railway station at Nowo Aidar and enemy troops and artillery in the Priwolnoje area. Three days later, the targets were columns on the Woroschilowgrad–Starobjelsk road and a railway bridge south of Petrowka. On the 6th, the Stuka and Fw 190 units of *Luftflotte* 4 were in action against Soviet artillery positions west of Krymskaya and east of Belgorod. Their efforts were successful.

To the opening of *Zitadelle*, I./Schl.G. 1 lost at least seven Fw 190s, although the *Gruppe* did claim six enemy aircraft shot down between 28 May and 24 June. The unit suffered its share of accidents too, including one that befell none other than Generaloberst von Richthofen's son, Wolf. On 18 May, the air fleet commander received a telephone call from Major Alfred Druschel, who served with the *Schlachtgeschwader*, to advise him that Wolf had suffered a crash in his Fw 190. 'He's been extremely lucky', von Richthofen noted in his

Fw 190A-4 'White F' of 5./Schl.G. 1, loaded with a centreline SC 250 bomb, is captured in flight over Ukraine in early 1943. The aircraft features the *Staffel* emblem of a bear carrying a machine gun and a damaged enemy tank over its shoulder, as well as the black triangle marking of the *Schlachtflieger*, which was used until April 1943 (*EN Archive*)

Four of the most accomplished *Schlachtflieger* and Knight's Cross-holders pose for a photograph in the southern Soviet Union in September 1942. They are, from left to right, Oberleutnant Georg Dörffel, *Staffelkapitän* 5./Schl.G. 1, Hauptmann Alfred Druschel, *Kommandeur* I./Schl.G. 1, Leutnant Josef Menapace, II./Schl.G. 2, and Oberleutnant Heinz Frank, *Staffelkapitän* 3./Schl.G. 1. This shot may have been taken at around the time of Druschel's award of the Oak Leaves on 3 September (*EN Archive*)

diary. 'He had an engine problem after take-off and ploughed into two buildings'. The younger von Richthofen suffered concussion and was ordered to take eight days' rest, but remained with his unit.

The scale of the battlefields in the Soviet Union was vast, but so were the potential targets. In general terms, the Luftwaffe foresaw the *Schlacht* units being used at both 'tactical' and 'strategic' levels. At a 'tactical' level, this meant conducting missions over the battle zone – usually an area of approximately 30 km in depth. Targets included infantry, their shelters and bunkers, field headquarters and command positions, communications and observation posts, supply dumps (weapons, ammunition, fuel, food), gun batteries (moving or dug in), tanks (mobile or stationary), vehicle columns (mobile and stationary) and vehicle parks, troop movements and assemblies (either on open ground or in buildings or woods), bridges, boats, railway stations and railway traffic (moving or troops and vehicles detraining).

At a 'strategic' level, this included – if possible – a target framework beyond direct coordination with ground forces, or targets which represented the materiel and personnel potential of the enemy.

In terms of ordnance, against ground troops in open country or in positions with little cover, the *Schlachtflieger* usually dropped lighter-weight, thicker-walled *Splitterbomben* (splinter/fragmentation and anti-personnel bombs) of SD-1, -2, -4 and -10 types, in each case the number denoting the bomb's weight in kilogrammes. The SD-1 bomb, for example, weighed 0.76 kg, had an explosive weight of 0.11 kg and was intended to be dropped using *Abwurfbehälter* ('AB' bomb containers).

The actual method of attack depended on target area conditions such as enemy AA fire and fighters, weather, and the types of weapons and/or ordnance to be used. In cases where AA fire and fighters would not be a consideration, generally the most effective type of attack was the shallow dive when dropping bombs and a low-level attack when strafing. The height for release of ordnance was determined by the type(s) of bombs being deployed – especially when using AB containers from which large clusters of fragmentation and anti-personnel bombs (for example, SD-1 or SD-2) were released and which required greater areas of dispersion.

A favoured ordnance of the Fw 190 *Schlachtflieger* was the *Abwurfbehälter* or 'AB' series of bomb containers. Seen here is an AB 250 container loaded with ten-kilogramme SD 10 *Splitterbomben* (fragmentation bombs). Intended for use against 'softer', unarmoured targets and light gun batteries and airfield surfaces, the SD series was armed with the eAZ (66) super-fast impact fuse. Up to 28 bombs could be loaded into an AB 250 (*EN Archive*)

Often, a pilot had to search for priority targets over the battlefield, but it was common for them to be well camouflaged. This forced a pilot to fly at altitudes from which only a shallow dive or low-level run was possible.

Designed for use against both humans and unarmoured vehicles, the SD-2 (known to the Allies as the 'butterfly bomb') contained 0.225 kg of Fp 60/40 explosive (60 per cent trinitrotoluene (TNT) and 40 per cent ammonium nitrate). Fusing was by means of a clockwork timer or a *Störzünder* 'harassment' fuse. When dropped from AB containers, SD-1s and SD-2s created 'bomb carpets' and had a considerable destructive effect. Such bombs, and bombs up to ten kilogrammes in weight, were also used against airfields in missions which were considered to be in indirect support of the Wehrmacht. These missions were intended to destroy dispersed enemy aircraft.

Although higher weight *Splitterbomben* of 50–70 kg were found to be less effective operationally, even with projecting fuses to make them explode above the ground, they were used because of their wider availability. For operations against horse-drawn and armoured vehicles, field fortifications and houses and towns where headquarters buildings were known to exist, it was usual to expend standard 250-kg *Splitterbomben* or HE types.

A worthy target for the Fw 190 units was the Soviet railway network, especially in instances during the movement of Red Army forces to and from front areas. Favoured targets were railway lines in and out of stations, and sections of line that could be easily blocked such as those leading to bridges and in cuttings. By comparison, attacks on open stretches of line and unoccupied stations resulted in little beneficial effect. These targets were usually attacked with 250-kg bombs, while troops climbing aboard or disembarking from trains were strafed and bombed with small *Splitterbomben*.

Increasingly, the *Schlachtgruppen* were called upon to destroy bridges, but they proved to be difficult targets and attacks by Fw 190s brought little success. Stone or concrete bridges needed direct hits from heavy bombs, and even then, results were often only temporary. Complete collapsing of bridges was almost impossible. Steel bridges were the hardest to inflict damage upon, since the blast effect caused by the generally lighter bombs carried by the *Schlachtgruppen* usually dissipated through the steelwork. Temporary military bridges and pontoons were attacked with a range of bombs from ten to 500 kg, but even so, often only brief interruption in enemy traffic flow could be achieved. With pontoon bridges, repairs could be affected quite quickly and easily.

When AA batteries were known to be present, elements of an Fw 190 formation would fly ahead to suppress the enemy gun crews, using AB containers loaded with one-kilogramme anti-personnel bombs so that the greater part of the formation could carry out the main attack with as little interference or jeopardy as possible. In instances where it was not possible to suppress the AA fire sufficiently, sharper diving attacks would have to be employed.

But in one respect, the Fw 190 as a *Schlacht* aircraft was stymied from the start. Even before operations commenced, there was a shortage of key ammunition. At a conference of RLM

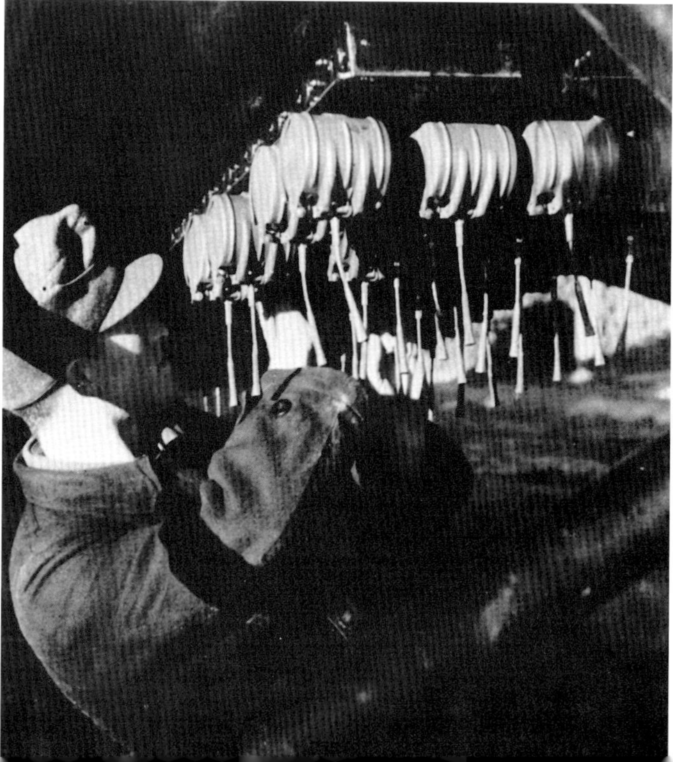

A Luftwaffe armourer secures a load of SD 2 *Splitterbomben* to a night ground-attack He 46. Known as 'butterfly bombs' on account of their opening *Bremsflügel* (brake vanes), they were used by Fw 190s to pepper airfields and also against 'softer' targets such as troop concentrations and the crews of light gun batteries. Highly dangerous to personnel, they were fitted with a *Störzünder* (deterrent fuse) which acted as a mine (*EN Archive*)

and Luftwaffe supply chiefs on 9 February 1943, the *Generalluftzeugmeister*, Generalfeldmarschall Erhard Milch, who had recently returned from an emergency posting to the Stalingrad sector, had been in no doubt that what was needed was more anti-personnel bombs – lots of them;

'There is a great shortage of one-kilogramme bombs in the field. What are the targets that make the employment of this bomb more than rewarding? The Russians are advancing across rear areas in thick columns. These people drive in three columns, with horses and horse-driven vehicles, three vehicles side by side. The infantry marches cross-country in small groups of 10, 20 or 40 men, widely dispersed. One cannot achieve any results with heavy bombs. If we had small bombs, we could pelt these people with them.

'Once the snow has melted – it is already thinning – we can achieve great results with the one-kilogramme. The 50-kg bomb has advantages over the one-kilogramme bomb only if we need to pierce armour or guns or underground shelters or similar installations. For these we must use the 50-kg bomb and upwards, but for the many mass targets, the destruction of which is decisive for the course of operations, we have to employ one-kilogramme bombs. If we can catch them with small bombs, this would be a major achievement. The Russians will try to attack all summer; either they will advance, or we advance and they retreat. Then we hit them with small bombs so that they lose the will to fight.

'*Luftflotte* 4 and Generaloberst von Richthofen have stated that they could drop *350,000* bombs per day – the total production – and von Richthofen is always asking for things and never getting anything. The production figure seems far too low. In addition, there are no reserve stocks available so that bombs cannot be distributed to the various fronts.'

In late June, Hitschhold departed to be replaced by Major Alfred Druschel as *Kommodore* of Schl.G. 1. Druschel, the son of a civil engineer and provincial official from Bindsachsen in Upper Hessen, joined the Luftwaffe in 1936, initially training as a bomber crew observer before attending a course as a *Luftflotte* staff officer. He transferred to SFG 10 (see Chapter One) in July 1938 and subsequently to II.(*Schlacht*)/LG 2, with whom he flew the Hs 123 with distinction in Poland, France and the Balkans before transferring to 2./Sch.G.1.

Druschel enjoyed the reputation of being a first-class pilot and something of a daredevil, and was appointed *Kommandeur* of I./Schl.G. 1 on 13 January 1942. He received the Knight's Cross on 21 August 1941, having flown 200 missions and claimed seven aerial victories. With Schl.G. 1, he was operational over the northern and southern sectors of the Eastern Front and was, as Hauptmann Druschel, awarded the Oak Leaves on 3 September 1942, having flown 600 missions. On 19 February 1943, he received the Swords, one of only seven dive-bomber and ground-attack pilots to be so awarded.

At the beginning of July, Hauptmann Georg Dörffel's I./Schl.G. 1 reported 52 Fw 190A-5s on strength along with some 20 F-3s. In the skies above what became a titanic battle of armour at Kursk, that month saw the Focke-Wulfs deployed in numbers against Soviet tanks. They would be loaded with AB 500 containers holding SD-2 fragmentation bombs, with which they attacked infantry positions and columns, as well as AA gun positions often in the process of digging in and setting up. Deployed ahead of II. *SS-Panzerkorps*, Fw 190s and Hs 123s would fly in coordinated operations with the Hs 129s of 4.(Pz) and 8.(Pz)/Schl.G. 1, which would aim for Soviet armour using their 30 mm MK 103 cannon.

Four Focke-Wulfs (three A-5s and an F-3) from I. *Gruppe* were lost or damaged on 5 July, including the A-5 of Oberleutnant Ernst Zielke of 2. *Staffel* whose aircraft turned over when landing and was written off. Two others also crashed, and another was shot down by AA fire, which also claimed two F-3s from II./Schl.G. 1.

On 7 July, heavy fighting took place between *Waffen*-SS units advancing towards Korocha and strong formations of T-34 and KV-1 tanks. The Fw 190s of Schl.G. 1 were sent in as well as Hs 129s, and after an intense two hours the Luftwaffe was successful in beating off the Soviet armour. The following afternoon, Fw 190s of I./Schl.G. 1 carrying AB 500s attacked concentrations of Red Army troops in open terrain west of the Korocha woods. As *Führer der Panzerjäger* (commander of the Hs 129-equipped anti-tank units) Hauptmann Bruno Meyer noted;

'It was like watching a sinister steamroller moving forwards. Even after the first aircraft had gone home and the next [Hs 129] *Staffel* dropped its bombs into the masses, they still did not stop their march but moved on without taking defensive action or seeking any cover. Only when the Fw 190s started mowing down their first ranks with cannon and machine gun fire and bombs began to fall on the outskirts of the woods to the west did this steamroller slowly grind to a halt.'

The Fw 190s of I./Schl.G. 1 were soon moved from the southern part of the bulge north to Orel to respond to another Soviet counter-offensive. Such was the intensity of operations that the *Gruppe* lost at least eight Fw 190s between 8 July and 2 August, although it also accounted for the destruction of several Il-2s and LaGG-3s in air combat around Belgorod.

The Fw 190s of the *Schlachtgruppen* were frequently involved in combat against enemy aircraft, and this was where the Focke-Wulf offered a significant benefit over the Ju 87. As Hitschhold explained in a post-war report for Allied Intelligence;

'On the Eastern Front it was usually sufficient if part of the ground-attack formation took over the fighter escort for the rest of the mission. It was even possible to use bomb-carrying Fw 190s as fighter escorts. This was done in the following way: at the beginning of the attack, one part of the formation stayed at altitude and furnished fighter cover. This part was then relieved by another part of the formation which had already dropped its bombs. The top cover then went down to conduct its own ground attacks. In case of contact with the enemy, bombs had to be jettisoned, with fuses armed if over enemy territory.'

In what is probably a training session, groundcrew work on the BMW 801 engine of an Fw 190A, probably of Schl.G. 1. Note the top of the tank of a fuel bowser in the lower part of the photograph. The aircraft has been fitted with an ER 4 supplementary bomb rack, which carries four SC 50 bombs (*Robert Forsyth Collection*)

By the end of July, of 71 aircraft reported on strength on 30 June, I./Schl.G. 1 had lost 16 Fw 190s in combat and 14 to accidents, with a further 13 undergoing repair, leaving operational strength at 28 aircraft.

Over 2–3 July, II./Schl.G. 1 was also pulled north from the Kuban to Varvarovka to strike at enemy forces along the Donets south of Kharkov, but the *Gruppe* was not used directly (or it was used only indirectly on a limited basis) in support of *Zitadelle* until early August, by which time the German initiative had been blunted. Nevertheless, as with I. *Gruppe*, in addition to ground-attack operations, II./Schl.G. 1 did shoot down enemy aircraft.

Of 59 Fw 190A-5s and F-3s on strength at the end of June, II./Schl.G. 1 had suffered 14 Focke-Wulfs lost in combat and 15 to accidents, with six undergoing repairs, resulting in an operational strength of 24 aircraft.

On 29 July, however, the *Gruppe* was once again moved south, to Rostov, where its Fw 190s were deployed against a Soviet armoured thrust along the Mius River. Just three days later, on 1 August, in a reflection of its 'fire brigade' status, the unit returned to Varvarovka. Here, a number of its Focke-Wulfs were destroyed in a Soviet bombing raid on its airfield. After that, the *Gruppe* pulled back to Rudka, from where it flew many missions supporting the defence of Kharkov. That city fell on 22 August, by which time II./Schl.G. 1 had suffered heavy losses. Six days later, the *Gruppe* moved to Stalino-Nord, continuing to fly support missions for German forces fighting around Kharkov, with the main target being Soviet armour.

Orel was taken by the Red Army on 4 August, and under subsequent enemy pressure, I./Schl.G. 1 was pulled back to Karachev and then to Bryansk. It continued flying missions, however, again claiming the destruction of enemy assets not only on the ground but also in the air, which says much for the 'multi-tasking' skill and tenacity of the *Schlachtflieger*.

The pilot of Fw 190A-5 'Green C' from *Stab* I./Schl.G. 1 watches from his cockpit as an armourer loads ammunition for his aircraft's port side MG 151/20 wing cannon. Another armourer approaches carrying a 50-kg bomb – no mean feat of strength! (*EN Archive*)

In a measure of recognition of this, in August 1943, the *Oberkommando der Luftwaffe* (OKL – Luftwaffe High Command) decided to unite the various types of ground-attack unit under one command, creating the post of *General der Schlachtflieger*. This command would oversee procurement, supply, training and tactics for the somewhat disparate Stuka, *Schlacht*, *Schnellkampf* (fast-bomber), *Jabo*, *Störkampf* (nuisance/harassment), *Panzerjäger* (anti-tank) and some *Zerstörer* (destroyer) units tasked with carrying out close-support missions on all battlefronts. The man chosen for the job was newly promoted Oberstleutnant Dr. Ernst Kupfer.

A qualified lawyer with chiselled features and a glacial set to his face, Kupfer was a very experienced and highly respected Stuka pilot and commander. He had seen combat over Greece and Crete as *Staffelkapitän* of 3./StG 2 and then from the opening of *Barbarossa* in the USSR, where, as *Kommandeur* of the new II./StG 2, he led his Ju 87s in support of 6. *Armee* as it advanced towards Stalingrad. In 1943, having been appointed *Kommodore* of his *Geschwader* in February of that year, Kupfer commanded his Stukas over the Crimea as they supported 17. *Armee.* In July, he was in action over Kursk, and by the conclusion of the failed German offensive there, he had flown 636 missions in just two-and-a-half years. Kupfer had been decorated with the Oak Leaves to the Knight's Cross by Hitler in early 1943.

Soon after taking up his position of *General der Schlachtflieger*, Kupfer met with Generalfeldmarschall Milch on 10 September, to whom he delivered a radical verbal report in which he put forward his views on the continuing use of dive-bombing. Kupfer believed that dive-bombing and the notion of 'a Ju 87 screaming down in a more or less vertical dive on its target' had had its day. Dive-bombing *had* been possible at times when the Luftwaffe enjoyed air supremacy such as in Poland, France and the Balkans, and when AA fire had not been such a threat. But on the Eastern Front and in North Africa these conditions no longer applied. Kupfer was blunt. 'Under no circumstances can we justify the continued employment of the Ju 87 – in the East or anywhere else'.

He told Milch that StG 2 had lost 89 of its crews in just eight months. 'This represents a yearly average of 100 per cent. If we keep on this way, it will mean the end of the dive-bomber units'.

Furthermore, the policy of sending out fighter escorts with the Stukas as had happened in the Kuban, at Orel and in North Africa, where on occasions 20 fighters were sent out with 20 Ju 87s, was – given the fighter procurement situation – 'ridiculous'.

Kupfer knew that the immediate solution lay in the Fw 190;

'We need an aeroplane which is flexible, fast and small enough to be hard to hit, and we need it in sufficient quantity for effective employment.

'For ground-support operations, then, the single-seater fighter aircraft is the best possible choice. I might point out that the single-seater, single-engined fighter has always been our most up-to-date aircraft model. One important step might be the modification of the fighter aircraft as a *Schlacht* aircraft, or fighter-bomber, by providing better visibility towards the rear and to the ground by means of periscopes or some such instrument. We could also use a better sighting device. We can only use as much outside armour as will have no effect on speed and manoeuvrability – the pilot will soon get rid of any plating which will slow him down in these respects.

'In addition, we need an air-to-ground radio to enable us to maintain contact with the ground forces, including tank units. Especially in cases where ground headquarters occupy advance positions, it is becoming increasingly important that there be some method of guiding the *Schlachtflugzeug* from the ground.'

Kupfer also wanted clear definitions in terms of nomenclature to avoid confusion both within the Luftwaffe and the Wehrmacht – a vital prerequisite at the front;

'The concepts of the *Jagdbomber* and *Schnellbomber* must no longer be used in my theatre of command. There are *Schlachtflugzeuge* and *Schlachtgeschwadern*. The other terms merely lead to confusion. I shall request the Reichsmarschall to rechristen these units "*Schlachtgeschwadern*".'

Oberst Dr. Ernst Kupfer, a former *Kommodore* of StG 2, was the first *General der Schlachtflieger* and the driving force behind the reorganisation of the Luftwaffe's ground-attack units in late 1943. He recognised that in a rapidly changing war, the days of the Ju 87 were numbered, and that the Fw 190 should be its successor. He did not live long enough to see the fruits of his initiative – Kupfer died in an He 111 crash in Greece on 6 November 1943 (*EN Archive*)

At the end of Kupfer's presentation Milch was displeased with the proposals, insisting that there was a marked difference between *Schlacht* units and the Stuka and *Panzerjagd* units. For some time Milch's view had been that while there was a need for an armoured aircraft able to operate over the battlefield, the Fw 190 would not be the aircraft to destroy tanks with bombs. A technical officer from Göring's staff who was also present at the meeting pointed out that the Reichsmarschall 'did not wish to abolish use of the term "Stuka"'.

Nevertheless, Kupfer had not only sowed the seed of change, but it was his presentation that led, within just a few weeks, to a reorganisation and redesignation of the Stuka and *Schlacht* units on the basis that the Fw 190 would replace the Ju 87.

Meanwhile, despite harbouring an offensive air war doctrine which favoured a short conflict with a favourable outcome brought about by sheer force, ironically, it was this very doctrine which had a negative influence on the development and employment of the *Schlachtflieger* and their units. In order to maximise force, it was often the case that the Luftwaffe either chose, or was forced to use, various inappropriate types of aircraft in the ground-attack role simply to achieve short-term gains or to ensure battlefield success.

It was the opinion of Generalmajor Hubertus Hitschhold, Kupfer's successor as *General der Schlachtflieger* and the Luftwaffe's last, that a neglect of strategic bombing resulted in, for example, even He 111 bombers being called upon for close-support missions. Hitschhold felt this to be a 'cardinal error' which 'had a bad effect on the development of the *Schlachtflieger*' resulting in increasingly adverse situations on the Eastern Front. From mid-1943 onwards, this meant that when it came to the *Schlachtgruppen* there were rarely any 'clear ideas', and thus the Ju 87 dive-bomber continued to be regarded as the primary and most effective 'ground-attack' aircraft even when dive-bombing had become largely ineffective.

Indeed, in September 1943, immediately after replacing Jeschonnek as Chief of General Staff, *General der Flieger* Günther Korten believed that a reorganised and dedicated strategic bomber force 'would provide more effective support for the Army than attacks against enemy ground forces on the field of battle'. Korten's logic was founded on the fact that the Wehrmacht suffered from a shortage of anti-tank weapons in the face of unexpectedly large numbers of Soviet tanks.

Since 1941, the Red Army had been building many of its tanks in factories far to the east, beyond the Urals, at centres such as Nizhny Tagil, Sverdlovsk, Chelyabinsk and Omsk, way beyond the range of German bombers. Therefore, it became the Luftwaffe's task to destroy Soviet armour in, as *General der Flieger* Paul Deichmann described it post-war, a 'painful piecemeal effort against heavy air defences on the battlefield, killing off [the threat] tank by tank'. Korten further felt that any delay incurred in close-support for the Wehrmacht as a result of a mass re-equipping of the Stuka units with the Fw 190 would simply have to be accepted.

In a report prepared for the Allies in October 1945, Hitschhold lamented that, 'The office of *General der Schlachtflieger*, and with it the combining of the ground-attack and dive-bomber units under one *Waffengeneral*, did not take place until too late'. According to Hitschhold, this resulted in a lack of coordination in tactics, training, planning and attempts at expansion. *Schlacht* operations were controlled by staffs with officers who lacked direct, practical experience of ground-attack work, and thus the maximum potential of the *Schlachtverbände* was never realised. Furthermore, because of the relatively low numbers of experienced ground-attack officers, it was difficult to rectify this.

By early September, I./Schl.G. 1 was in northern Ukraine to strike at enemy armour heading towards Kiev, where Soviet AA fire continued to be a nemesis for the *Schlachtflieger*. On 4 September, Hauptmann Johannes 'Jonny' Meinecke, the Austrian *Staffelkapitän* of 1./Schl.G. 1 and a former *Fallschirmjäger*, was downed in his Fw 190A-6 by AA guns near Bresinov while making a transfer flight. Meinecke had been awarded the Knight's Cross on 7 April 1943 after having flown 400 missions.

The *Gruppe* continued to absorb pilot and aircraft losses (to both its A- and F-models). Meinecke's successor as head of 1. *Staffel*, fellow Austrian and Stalingrad veteran Hauptmann Josef Menapace, became another victim as he attacked Soviet forces advancing southwest from Nezhin. All losses were hard to bear, but in the case of 'Bazi' Menapace, it would very probably have hit unit morale badly.

An old hand, having flown the Hs 123 with II.(*Schlacht*)/LG 2 in Greece in 1941, Menapace had completed 300 missions by early January 1942. In May of that year, he and his *Staffel* saw action over Kharkov, and Menapace's reports on enemy dispositions during the fighting around the city had been appreciated by Wehrmacht commanders. He was appointed *Staffelkapitän* of 7.(*Schlacht*)/LG 2 on 31 July 1942, by which time he had chalked up 600 missions. Menapace was decorated with the Knight's Cross on 20 August 1942 after 650 missions.

On 6 October 1943, just days after taking command of 1./Schl.G. 1, Menapace made his first flight in an Fw 190. While undertaking a mission over Stracholessje, to the south of the Pripyat Marshes and on the edge of the Dnipro River, his Focke-Wulf was hit by AA fire and crashed in flames. By the time of his death, Menapace had flown more than 700 missions in the Hs 123.

As mentioned, II./Schl.G. 1's contribution to the Wehrmacht's battlefield awareness was greatly valued. This meant that not only were the Fw 190 *Schlachtflugzeuge* flying close-support and ground-attack missions, but also

A member of the groundcrew sits on the starboard wing of the Fw 190A-6 of Hauptmann Johannes Meinecke of I./Schl.G. 1 in order to assist the pilot as he taxies out. Forward vision from the cockpit of the aircraft was compromised by the size of the engine cowling. Meinecke served as *Gruppe* Technical Officer (hence the fuselage 'T') and, subsequently, as *Staffelkapitän* of 1./Schl.G. 1. A veteran of Stalingrad, he was awarded the Knight's Cross on 7 April 1943. Meinecke was killed during a ferry flight when his Fw 190 was hit by AA fire northeast of Kiev on 4 September 1943 (*EN Archive*)

acting as local reconnaissance, relaying their observations of Soviet tank and troop movements back to the intelligence staffs of the *Fliegerdivision* and *Fliegerkorps*. However, the consensus among the *Schlachtflieger* at this time was one of increasing enemy strength and a thin and over-stretched German front.

In early September 1943 II./Schl.G. 1 pulled back to Kiev-Süd, where the *Gruppe* had a brief period of rest while its Fw 190s received a badly needed overhaul, although the unit simultaneously carried out ground-attack missions against enemy armour heading towards Kiev. Oberfeldwebel Hermann Buchner was an Austrian-born pilot serving with 6./Schl.G. 1 at this time, and he remembered;

'From Stalino, we again flew against tanks and accompanying infantry which had broken through the lines. The tanks were our prime target. We *Schlachtflieger* with our robust Fw 190s were needed everywhere, and with our on-board weapons and bombs, we achieved good success. However, there were too few of us and the enemy's superior strength was too great.'

The planned conversion of the Ju 87 units to the Fw 190 progressed slowly, chiefly because of the demand placed on production for the fighter variant to supply the Reich defence fighter units. By 18 October 1943, however, a reorganisation of the *Schlacht* arm had taken place in line with Kupfer's aims and vision for a more streamlined force of '*Schlachtgeschwadern*' which would carry the new, abbreviated nomenclature of 'SG'. Of the original Fw 190-equipped *Schlacht* units, 1./Schl.G 1 was disbanded, 2. and 3./Schl.G 1 became the new 5. and 6./SG 77, while 5., 6. and 7./Schl.G 1 were redesignated 8., 6. and 7./SG 2, respectively.

Also, 1., 2. and 3./Schl.G 2 which, since being equipped with the Fw 190 in April 1943, had been in Sicily and mainland Italy (see Chapter Four), were redesignated 1., 2. and 3./SG 10, while 5., 6. and 7./Schl.G 2 became, respectively, 4./SG 2, 3./SG 4 and 3./SG 2 (1. and 2./SG 4 were newly established *Staffeln*). The Hs 129-equipped 4.(Pz) and 8.(Pz)/Schl.G. 1 were redesignated 10. and 11.(Pz)/SG 9.

In terms of the Ju 87 dive-bomber *Gruppen*, all were redesignated and would take on the Fw 190 at different times during 1944, as would the Fw 190-equipped fast-bomber *Gruppen* II. and III./SKG 10, which became II. and III./SG 4, while IV./SKG 10 became II./SG 10.

With little in the way of attrition replacements reaching the frontline, it was fortunate that the serviceability levels within the Fw 190-equipped *Schlachtgruppen* remained generally very high – usually between 70–80 per cent. To a great extent this was due to the fact that the Focke-Wulf was easier to service than many other aircraft.

Despite battlefield successes and the resilience of the Fw 190 as a *Schlachtflugzeug*, it seemed Göring remained unconvinced by its operational record. He revealed his view on the subject at a meeting with Milch on 28 October, to whom he remarked, 'A fighter-bomber is a fighter that makes a virtue out of necessity'.

But it is evident from surviving documents that by late 1943, the Luftwaffe viewed the use of 'strategic' air units – in other words, its twin-engined medium bomber units – in ground-support operations as wasteful. As one report noted, a result of the continuing use of the Luftwaffe in direct support of the Wehrmacht was 'the unnecessary employment of valuable and highly trained [bomber] crews. Knowledge and skill acquired in long and costly training in navigation and long-range bombing is, by the very nature of ground-attack operations, completely wasted. Not only is navigational dexterity and practice lost on missions where only visual observation is necessary (the crew knows its own sector of the front and there is no necessity, and often no opportunity, for complex navigational methods), but mental aptitude is also very often diminished'.

The report stressed;

'The ground-attack pilot has the task of attacking enemy positions, salients and even infantry and tanks with bombs and cannon fire. The aircraft designed for strategic bombing are unsuited to such missions. Bombs dropped from a great height can only be used successfully if a saturation attack is made, and in any case, recognition of small targets is difficult from such an altitude. If employed on low-level attacks, these bombers, even when protected by fighters, suffer losses altogether disproportionate to the success which they achieve.

'Aircraft specially designed for this type of combat, such as the Fw 190, are necessary, and these can operate without fighter escort. The Ju 87 cannot even be considered for ground-strafing purposes in view of its low speed and the formidable Flak and fighter defences now encountered. The Reichsmarschall has ordered that its production be discontinued and replaced by that of Fw 190s.

'Urgent consideration should therefore be given to the problem of whether a number of Fw 190s originally intended for use as fighters should not be allocated as ground-attack aircraft with a view to building up a strong ground-attack force for the following purposes:

1. To help the Army in its difficult defensive struggle and its later offensive campaigns with the best weapon available at the present time (Fw 190).
2. To free bomber crews as soon as possible for their own tasks.
3. To employ aircraft which are costly to produce and ill-suited for ground-attack more reasonably and in a way more compatible with their possibilities than has been done hitherto.'

This illustrates, beautifully, the dilemma facing the German command – it could not sacrifice bombers and their highly trained crews in 'wasteful' ground-attack missions, but the Luftwaffe could ill afford to divert delivery of Fw 190s away from the vital need for the daylight air defence of the homeland against the USAAF's bombing raids in favour of dangerous *Schlacht* operations in the East. But paradoxically, a Luftwaffe instruction from autumn 1943 aimed at units operating in the Soviet Union stated that, 'Stukas must have strong fighter cover, or else be employed in mixed formations with Fw 190 *Schlachtflugzeuge*'.

The cause of the *Schlachtflieger* was bolstered to some extent in October 1943 when Major Druschel was appointed *Inspizient der Tag-Schlachtfliegerverbände beim General der Schlachtflieger* (Inspector of Daylight *Schlacht* Units for the *General der Schlachtflieger*). Druschel's considerable combat experience would no doubt be a bonus to Kupfer and his staff, although unfortunately their working relationship would be short-lived.

On 6 November 1943, while on an inspection tour of Stuka units in Greece, the He 111 in which Kupfer was travelling crashed in mountains south of the Greek–Macedonian border. Kupfer's body, along with others in the crew, was found 11 days later. It remained to be seen how the reorganisation of the *Schlacht* units and the greater use of the Fw 190 as a ground-attack aircraft would play out in the decisive year that lay ahead for the Third Reich.

CHAPTER FOUR

THE SOUTH – 1942–43

A groundcrewman in customary northern European black overalls guides an Fw 190 from an unidentified unit carrying four underwing 50-kg bombs at an airfield in North Africa or Italy (*EN Archive*)

From November 1942, the Axis military position in North Africa became increasingly perilous. Generalfeldmarschall Erwin Rommel, commander of the *Afrika Korps*, used all his tactical dexterity to pull his men westwards, away from defeat after his lines had been broken by the British Eighth Army on 4 November at what became known as the Second Battle of El Alamein. By the 11th, Axis forces had left Egypt, and on the 13th, further along the coast, Tobruk, in Libya, was abandoned. Both events immediately followed a month of ever-diminishing fuel supply for the *Deutsch-Italienische Panzerarmee* as it fought to hold on to Cyrenaica. The Royal Air Force (RAF) had also attained air superiority over the coast as far as the Gulf of Sidra.

Furthermore, from 8 November, Operation *Torch* had seen the Allies commit more than 100,000 men to an invasion of French North Africa which was intended, fundamentally, to get US ground forces into the war there. If, metaphorically, there had ever been a stake driven into the heart of the Axis North African war effort, then that had been it.

The Luftwaffe struggled, with dwindling supplies of aircraft, pilots, ammunition, equipment and airfields, to render support as best it could to the severely compromised German ground forces. In terms of crucial tactical air support, resources were slender. On 20 November, the Luftwaffe's main tactical command in-theatre, *Fliegerführer Afrika*, reported 194 pilots on its strength, of which the ground-attack force numbered 35 Ju 87 dive-bomber pilots (18 ready) and 24 *Schlachtflieger*, of whom just five were ready for operations. This force included the Ju 87s of StG 3, the recently arrived Bf 109 *Jabos* of I./Schl.G. 2 and the Hs 129s of 4.(Pz.)/Schl.G. 2, the latter plagued by problems with their engine air filters.

Additionally, an Fw 190 *Jabo* unit, III. *Gruppe* of *Zerstörergeschwader* (ZG) 2 under Hauptmann Wilhelm Hachfeld and equipped with 20 Fw 190A-4s, arrived at Sidi Ahmed airfield (Bizerta) on the northern Tunisian coast on 15 November, where it was attached to II./JG 53. But the appearance of III./ZG 2 did not herald the Focke-Wulf's debut in North Africa.

That accolade went to small test unit *Erprobungskommando* (E.Kdo) 19, which had been formed at Castel Benito airfield near Tripoli on 1 July 1942. Its function was to test the Bf 109G and Fw 190 for their performances in tropical conditions as, respectively, fighter and *Jabo*/*Schlacht* types. The unit remained in existence for only some two to three months, and in terms of personnel, comprised two fighter instructors and six would-be fighter pilots drawn from the operational training *Gruppe*, *Ergänzungs-Jagdgruppe Süd* at Villacoublay, in France, which fed pilots to JGs 27 and 53 in North Africa.

Unfortunately, little is known of E.Kdo 19's activities, although it is possible that the *Staffelkapitän* of 2./JG 27, Hauptmann Ernst Maack, may have been assigned as its commander. One known loss suffered by the *Kommando* was that of Leutnant Franz Elble from the *Erprobungsstelle* at Rechlin, who crashed in his Fw 190A-3 at Castel Benito on 19 July. One of the unit's aircraft was found at Al-Berka, Benghazi, by South African troops in the wake of the Allied breakthrough at El Alamein.

While not a *Schlacht* unit in terms of operational purpose or designation, it is necessary to include an account of the operations of III./ZG 2 (later III./SKG 10), as the *Gruppe* 'trailblazed' the Fw 190 in the ground-attack role in North Africa.

Formed at Parndorf in April 1942 under the aforementioned Hauptmann Hachfeld, the *Gruppe* was initially equipped with Bf 109E-7s. Dessau-born Hachfeld had flown the Bf 109 with I.(*Jagd*)/LG 2 over England in 1940 before joining 2./JG 51 in October of that year. Between then and serving in the USSR during the opening weeks of *Barbarossa*, Hachfeld became adept at devising *Jabo* tactics for the Bf 109, earning himself the moniker '*Bomben-Willi*'. He was appointed *Kommandeur* of I./JG 51 on 26 August, a position he held until May 1942 when he took command of III./ZG 2 at Parndorf, at which time it was equipped with Bf 109Gs.

The *Gruppe* then spent a brief period in the southern Soviet Union in the summer of 1942, flying ground-attack missions. Targets for the unit included troop concentrations, vehicle columns, armour and artillery positions. By the time it was relocated back to Parndorf III./ZG 2 had executed 844 sorties, during which it had accounted for 226 enemy vehicles and four tanks destroyed.

At Parndorf the unit converted to the Fw 190A-4 and then moved to Cognac, in France, where training commenced in both dive- and level bombing, as well as anti-shipping missions. The *Gruppe*'s training was deemed to be completed by mid-October, and one of its first tastes of combat as a *Jabo* unit was in a raid against Canterbury, in Kent, on 31 October. Only days later, however, Göring instructed that the Luftwaffe in North Africa should be bolstered by 40 Fw 190 fighter-bombers, and thus it was that, staging via mainland Italy and Sicily, III./ZG 2 arrived at Sidi Ahmed on 15 November, 20 Fw 190s short of Göring's requested number.

For the next five-and-a-half months, firstly as III./ZG 2 and then having been redesignated as a *Schnellkampfgruppe* (fast bomber *Gruppe*), the Fw 190s waged an intense war against the Allied forces in Tunisia and Algeria.

Throughout the latter half of November, 1942 Hachfeld's *Jabos* carried out regular missions commencing on the afternoon of the 16th, when 12 Fw 190s loaded with SC 250s attacked the British 36th Infantry Brigade, a lightly equipped force able to operate only some ten miles or so from its maintenance area. The Brigade was advancing along the coastal road from Bône when the Fw 190s struck east of Tabarka. Flying in the formation with Hachfeld that day were the *Staffelkapitäne* of 8./ZG 2, Hauptmann Hans-Jobst Hauenschild, and 9./ZG 2, Hauptmann Karl Preiser.

These two pilots, both former fighter instructors, brought some combat experience to the *Gruppe*. Hauenschild, like his *Gruppenkommandeur*, had flown with I.(*Jagd*)/LG 2 before joining JG 2 and then serving as an instructor at two schools prior to a stint with 6./JG 54. Preiser, formerly Technical Officer with II./JG 27, then spent time as a senior instructor with *Jagdfliegervorschule* 1.

On their debut in Tunisia, the Fw 190s dropped bombs on towed artillery and then strafed vehicles, leaving at least two on fire.

On 18 November, after having attacked shipping in Bône harbour the day before, III./ZG 2 destroyed more enemy transport vehicles. The following morning, amidst rain, Hachfeld led six Fw 190s against Allied artillery south of Djebel Abiod, two SC 500s landing on the target. That afternoon, as the weather cleared, Hauenschild led nine Focke-Wulfs, under escort from Bf 109s of II./JG 53, to attack vehicles on the road between Oued Zarga and Medjez-el-Bab. An SC 500 was dropped on an AA gun position and several strafing runs were carried out that left at least five trucks burning. The *Gruppe* had flown 27 sorties.

The 22nd was a busy day. In the early afternoon, nine Fw 190s, escorted by fighters from JG 53, attacked the Allied airfield at Souk el Arba, some 50 km inland, south of Tabarka. As the *Jabos* arrived over their target, a pair of Spitfires was spotted taking off, and these were engaged by the Bf 109s. Sweeping over the airfield, the Fw 190s dropped their bombs amongst what was estimated to be more than 20 Spitfires. Two of the British fighters exploded while in the process of refuelling – the German pilots claimed ten Spitfires destroyed and four damaged. One Spitfire pilot of No 72 Sqn recalled, 'Twelve 109s [sic] bombed and machine-gunned us at 1.30 p.m. Wiped out eight of our Spits. Was I scared, no cover'.

During their homeward flight, the *Jabos* strafed Allied vehicles, destroying two and damaging four.

Later that afternoon, despite deteriorating weather, Hauenschild was in the air at the head of a formation of ten Fw 190s heading back to Souk el Arba. One bomb landed directly on a Spitfire and others caused destruction or damage to parked aircraft. Once more, as the III./ZG 2 machines headed home, they left their 'calling card' on another column of trucks, destroying four and damaging a further 15 in a low-level strafing run. By the end of the day, the *Gruppe* had filed claims for 16 enemy aircraft destroyed and four damaged on the ground, along with six vehicles destroyed and 19 damaged.

While not particularly heavy blows in themselves, the attacks carried out by III./ZG 2 in its first missions would have come as a shock to the British, and forced a heightened sense of awareness on the part of the Fw 190 pilots flying over hostile and unfamiliar terrain.

However, the need for fighter escort for the Fw 190s was always a problem, as the Luftwaffe – already stretched to the limit – failed to gain air superiority over the Allies. It was an issue that would persist beyond Tunisia, as Hitschhold described;

'The prerequisite for successful and lasting operations of ground-attack units is air superiority. Wherever the Germans did not have air superiority, their ground-attack operations were almost ineffective. This lesson was confirmed in [North] Africa, in Italy and on the Western Front. In these places, suffering from high losses of aircraft, planned and effective support of ground operations was *not* achieved. A raising of the number of ground-attack units would only have been useful if air superiority could have been won back.'

That said, it could be viewed as an accomplishment that III./ZG 2 was able to inflict damage against the Allies at all. Its operations also proved that the Fw 190 *was* an effective ground-attack fighter *despite* enemy air superiority.

The tactical technique employed by the Fw 190 units in North Africa and, later, in Italy involved approaching a land target at an altitude of approximately 50 m (and by doing so, making the Focke-Wulf a smaller target for AA gunners). When at around 1.5 km from the target, the pilot made a shallow climb, levelling out at 300 m before then making a shallow dive, during which individual targets would be selected. Just prior to bomb release, the pilot would again level out, release his bomb and then exit in an evasive turn. Wherever possible, and in instances of light ground defence, the pilot would then turn for another strafing attack with guns.

Hauptmann Fritz Schröter, a *Jabo* pilot who flew Fw 190s in North Africa and Italy, recorded how, after making an attack, 'The return flight was made at low level and strafing attacks were carried out against vehicles. In such cases the unit would break up into *Schwärme* of four aircraft. Landing was carried out by one aircraft at a time, with one *Staffel* being ordered to stay over the airfield to provide cover for those landing'.

On several occasions, the fact that a number of III./ZG 2's pilots had fighter combat experience proved to be important. During the second mission of the day on 28 November, the *Gruppe* returned to Sidi Ahmed in time to intercept a bombing raid by

A British soldier peers into the armament compartment behind the BMW engine bulkhead of Fw 190A-5/U3 trop 'White D' of II./Schl.G. 2 in Tunisia in May 1943. Note the intake for the sand filter on the cowling, the empty port for the wing-mounted MG 151 cannon and the ER 4 rack suspended from the fuselage centreline rack. The Focke-Wulf's nose is adorned with the II. *Gruppe* emblem of Mickey Mouse riding a bomb and wielding an axe (*EN Archive*)

B-17s from the USAAF's Twelfth Air Force. As the bombers left the airfield, the Fw 190s set off in pursuit. Unteroffizier Franz-Josef Schlieker shot down a Flying Fortress of the 301st Bombardment Group, while Feldwebel Karl Golles accounted for a 'straggler' low over the sea.

Operations continued into December, but on the 2nd the *Gruppe* suffered its first pilot loss, and it was a significant one. At 1030 hrs, Hauptmann Hachfeld commenced his take-off run along with seven other Focke-Wulfs on the first mission of the day, but as he did so his Fw 190A-3 ran into another from II./JG 2, which had also recently arrived in Tunisia. Unteroffizier Adolf Dilg of III./ZG 2 recalled;

'It was one of those silly accidents, well clear of the enemy, which have claimed so many aces. He had just begun his take-off run for an attack on an enemy position when he collided with another Fw 190 which had just landed and stopped on the runway. Hachfeld's Focke-Wulf nosed over on to its back and caught fire. He was dead before the rescue team could get him out. From outside our crewroom we watched with horror as the drama unfolded, unable to do anything to help.'

Despite any shock felt by Dilg and his comrades, III./ZG 2 undertook several sorties that day against targets in Tebourda, a town 40 km west of Tunis, and amongst other things left the railway station on fire.

Following the loss of Hauptmann Hachfeld, command of the *Gruppe* passed to Hauptmann Preiser. On or around 20 December, III./ZG 2 was redesignated III./SKG 10 – a more fitting redesignation given its combined fighter-bomber and ground-attack roles – with 7., 8. and 9./ZG 2 becoming 9., 10. and 11./SKG 10.

Under its new nomenclature, for the rest of 1942 and into the spring of 1943, the unit carried out an impressive range of operations. Initially, the focus was on fighter-bomber missions against 'fixed' targets such as harbour installations at Bône, enemy airfields in both Algeria and western Tunisia, road junctions and railway stations. From February 1943,

Luftwaffe mechanic Reinhold Omert stands next to Fw 190A-5/U3 trop 'White H' of 5./Schl.G. 2. The aircraft stands in a crude, low-walled blast pen made of sand, earth and stones (*Omert/Jessen*)

the target profile was shaped more by army and close support, as the ground fighting in Tunisia grew in its ferocity.

In the meantime, possibly because of Kupfer's initiatives and the efforts of Schl.G. 1 in the East, the decision was taken to form a new dedicated *Schlachtgeschwader* to be known as Schl.G. 2, with the aim of it being used primarily in the North African and Mediterranean theatres. Somewhat unusually, I. *Gruppe* was established before a *Geschwaderstab*, with orders for the *Gruppe*'s formation at Comiso, on Sicily, being issued on 28 September 1942.

I./Schl.G. 2 was created by the amalgamation of an ad-hoc grouping known as the '*Jabo-Gruppe Afrika*' and elements of III./ZG 1 which was in the process of converting from the Bf 109E-7/U1 to the problematic twin-engined Messerschmitt Me 210 at Trapani, with training in readiness being conducted on Bf 110s. I./Schl.G. 2 was stiffened by the additional inclusion of personnel from StG 3.

The '*Jabo-Gruppe Afrika*' was a composite tactical, semi-autonomous, fighter-bomber unit formed at the beginning of September 1942 and comprising elements drawn from 10.(*Jabo*)/JG 27 and 10.(*Jabo*)/JG 53. These elements formed, respectively, 2. and 1./Schl.G. 2, while those from III./ZG 1 provided the nucleus for a 3. *Staffel*. All these elements were initially under the command of the former *Staffelkapitän* of 10.(*Jabo*)/JG 53, Oberleutnant Hermann Langemann, before being assembled at Comiso in mid-October under a new *Gruppenkommandeur*, Hauptmann Johann Drescher.

A former Ju 87 pilot and *Staffelkapitän* of 3./StG 3, Drescher had experienced a lucky escape in late May 1942 when his Ju 87 was shot down over Egypt by RAF Kittyhawks. Drescher's Junkers force-landed in the Gazala area and he was captured, only to later escape from Allied captivity.

For its initial operations, I./Schl.G. 2 was equipped with Bf 109Es and then Fs, and from September 1942 to April 1943, it was engaged over Egypt, Libya and Tunisia, conducting *Jabo* raids against Malta, ground-attack missions around El Alamein, *Jabo* attacks on enemy airfields and operations over Kasserine. Then, in mid-April, it handed its remaining Messerschmitts to III./SKG 10 and departed Tunisia for Bari and then Brindisi, both in Italy, where it re-equipped with the Fw 190.

Fw 190A-5/U3 trop 'White B' of 5./Schl.G. 2 at an airfield in the Mediterranean in 1943. The fuselage is marked with a white Mediterranean Theatre recognition band (*EN Archive*)

It would not be until December 1942 that a *Stab* and II. *Gruppe* was established at Gleiwitz in Upper Silesia (although some sources state Deblin-Irena, 100 km south of Warsaw). Both formations formed up on Fw 190A-3/5s under the overall command of Hauptmann Wolfgang Schenck, receiving their first aircraft in February 1943.

Schenck was a very experienced unit commander and tactician. He returned from farming in East Africa to join the Luftwaffe in 1938 as a fighter pilot with II./JG 132. This *Gruppe* went through a series of redesignations, and by the time of the Polish campaign it had become I./ZG 1, with whom Schenck flew the Bf 110. Subsequently, he served in Poland and France, but was wounded in aerial combat and was hospitalised for three months. Upon his return to duties in September 1940, Schenck was assigned to *Erprobungsgruppe* 210, taking over command of 1. *Staffel* within weeks. Schenck conducted regular and highly effective fighter-bomber missions in the Bf 110 over southern England, targeting industrial areas and shipping (he accounted for 38,000 tons sunk).

In April 1941 Schenck's *Staffel* was redesignated 1./SKG 10 and subsequently saw action in the Soviet Union, where it operated with great success. On one occasion, during an attack by 1./SKG 10 on a Soviet airfield in the southern sector of the front, Schenck shot down four enemy aircraft and destroyed several more on the ground – a deed for which he would be awarded the Knight's Cross on 14 August 1941. This was followed by the Oak Leaves in October 1942, before he was withdrawn from operations to take up a position within the RLM. At the end of January 1943, he returned to operations as *Kommodore* of the new Schl.G. 2, but with relatively little experience on single-engined aircraft.

Appointed to lead II./Schl.G. 2 was Hauptmann Werner Dörnbrack, a veteran *Schlachtflieger* from Dortmund-Ering known as '*Prinzchen*' (Little Prince), who had commenced his operational flying with II.(Schl.)/LG 2 and with whom he saw service over Poland, France, the Channel Front, Greece and the USSR, for much of which he flew the Hs 123. He was awarded the Knight's Cross on 21 August 1941 after 200 missions and for his successes during operations in the Bjalystok area.

II./Schl.G. 2 numbered several instructor pilots from Luftwaffe flying schools recently trained to fly fighter-bomber missions, but this did not, necessarily, mean *Schlacht* missions. However, the *Staffelkapitäne* were experienced men, such as Oberleutnant Karl Langenberg, who led 5. *Staffel* and who had claimed seven aerial victories while flying Bf 110s with 5./ZG 76 in 1940, while at the head of 7./Schl.G. 2 was Oberleutnant Hans-Hennig von Prittwitz *und* Gaffron, a fluent French and Italian speaker who had flown *Jabo* missions in the East with 7./ZG 2.

Both the *Stab* and II./Schl.G. 2, which had been assigned 26 Fw 190 A-5/U-3s, reached Sidi Ahmed, via Italy, with just 17 such aircraft on 18 April 1943, having been posted in as relief for Langemann's departing I./Schl.G. 2. They arrived in a cauldron in which Axis forces were fighting with savage intensity to maintain a grip on North Africa. Already though, Gen Bernard Montgomery's Eighth Army was pushing up from the south, having overrun Wadi Akarit. The 'Desert Rats' had reached Enfidaville and were preparing to move on to the hills to the north. South of the coast, the US Army's II Corps was advancing to Mateur.

But for II./Schl.G. 2, its brief stay in Tunisia must have felt like swimming against an ever-strengthening tide. According to Dörnbrack, his *Gruppe's* task was to provide support for the *Afrika Korps* by mainly countering Allied armoured advances. Among II./Schl.G. 2's first targets on 20 April, however, were enemy airfields at La Marsa, La Sebala, Creteville and Protville.

A *Kette* of Fw 190s of 5./Schl.G. 2 fitted with ER 4 racks photographed during the unit's transfer flight to the Mediterranean in the spring of 1943 (*Petrick/Jessen*)

Allied radio intercepts of Luftwaffe signals indicate that orders were issued at this time for III./SKG 10 and II./Schl.G. 2 to withdraw their aircraft to Sicily each evening and to send over only the required number of machines to Tunisia each morning. Aside from the drain on precious fuel, this was not the most practical way to operate, as it tired pilots and limited combat time. Nevertheless, on the morning of the 21st, Fw 190s from II./Schl.G. 2 bombed vehicles on the road between Teboursouk and Medjez-el-Bab, with further such missions taking place in the afternoon.

At this time the *Gruppe* was operating with around 12 aircraft – a meagre amount – but it continued to maintain a respectable sortie rate. On the 25th, for example, it completed 43 in seven missions, inflicting a not inconsiderable 'nuisance' factor on Allied forces. However, that very evening, the unit lost some of its Fw 190s in a bombing raid on Sidi Ahmed.

On the 27th, II./Sch.G. 2 operated against armour and vehicles near Medjez-el-Bab, leaving tanks burning. Two days later the Fw 190s struck again, destroying 21 vehicles, an ammunition dump and a tank. On the 30th, escorted by Bf 109s from II./JG 53, Fw 190s from II./Sch.G. 2 took off to attack American tanks northwest of Medjez-el-Bab, but when no armour was sighted vehicles in the area were targeted instead.

By this stage, the situation facing the remaining German forces in Tunisia had become critical, and the decision had been taken to evacuate III./SKG 10 to Sicily – the *Gruppe* handed over four of its Fw 190A-5s to II./Sch.G. 2 before it left. But the Germans kept fighting, as the British military historian Kenneth Macksey commented. Even 'as the last week of April dragged to an end, no clear-cut signs of an Axis collapse could be detected by the Allies'.

Doggedly, against very adverse conditions, during the first few days of May II./Sch.G. 2 continued to operate. Werner Dörnbrack remembered how Sidi Ahmed and the other remaining landing grounds operated by the Luftwaffe were bombed on average three times a day. The *Gruppe* flew sorties around Tunis in an attempt to provide some air cover for evacuating German forces. On 8 May, the *Staffelkapitän* of 7./Sch.G. 2, Oberleutnant Siegfried Basse, suffered combat damage while over Tunis, and upon returning to his unit's landing ground at Menzel bou Zelfa, his Fw 190A-5 overturned and he was killed.

The Fw 190s of II./Sch.G. 2 flew their last missions from Cap Bon, the tip of Tunisia closest to Sicily. When combat operations were no longer possible, the Focke-Wulfs were used as emergency transports to fly the *Gruppe*'s groundcrews over to Sicily. This was achieved by the removal of all armour plating and radio equipment so that as many as four men could squeeze into the fuselage. It must have been a trepidatious experience to be in an Fw 190 overloaded with five men flying across the Mediterranean to Sicily, especially for those crammed into the dark fuselage. In addition to their own groundcrews, the Fw 190s also ferried men from other Luftwaffe units.

One Allied pilot summed things up for the Axis situation when he reported the previous month that, 'We have nothing to bomb. There are no enemy aircraft in the sky. There is practically nothing we can see to hit, nothing to strafe'.

On 13 May the last Axis forces surrendered in Tunisia. II./Sch.G. 2 had lost around 30 Fw 190A-5s in the fighting there.

For Sch.G. 2, the coming weeks would be a period of intensive operations and disruptive movement. By 21 May, Dörnbrack's II. *Gruppe*, with around 30 Fw 190s, was based on the airfields in the Gerbini area of eastern Sicily, and that day carried out a major early morning attack on enemy airfields on Malta. The mission was intended to be undertaken in close cooperation with Focke-Wulfs from III./SKG 10 and under escort provided by JG 53, but poor communication led to a breakdown of the cover for the Focke-Wulfs of that *Gruppe*. II./Sch.G. 2's aircraft, however, loaded variously with AB 500 containers and 500-kg bombs, pressed on with the benefit of escort from 22 Bf 109s of II./JG 53.

The *Gruppe*'s 28 Fw 190s reached Hal Far airfield on Malta, and amidst intense AA fire, dived down out of the sun, evading enemy fighters as they did so, but losing at least one of their number in the process when Feldwebel Otto Sorg of 5. *Staffel* went missing. Bombs were dropped on Hal Far and also on Takali airfield, after which the Fw 190s turned and headed back to Sicily at low level. For his part, Dörnbrack was unconvinced about the effect of his *Gruppe*'s attack, mainly because he felt his pilots remained 'unsure' of their aircraft, and that their numbers were too small to have any great impact against the defences of Malta.

A plus was that during May, Sch.G. 2's *Stab* and two *Gruppen* had taken delivery of 53 new Fw 190A-5s (U3s and U8s) and four F-3s, with further aircraft returning from repair and some arriving from other units. But by early June 1943, the writing was on the wall in the Mediterranean for the Axis, as the focus of Allied strategy fell on the taking of Sicily. For German forces, this meant another draining campaign of defence. On the 3rd, II./Sch.G. 2, again under escort from Bf 109s, attacked shipping off Cap Bon but results were inconclusive.

The focus of operations by the *Gruppe* then shifted to the tiny, fortified island of Pantelleria between Tunisia and Sicily, which the Allied command wanted taken as soon as possible to avoid any impediment to the landings on Sicily. It was envisaged that the island could also be used as a support base for further American operations, and so for the *Jabos* of III./SKG 10 and the *Schlachtflieger* of II./Sch.G. 2, a primary target at this time became Allied naval vessels south of Pantelleria. Five Fw 190s from II./Sch.G. 2 went out in the evening of 6 June to attack shipping but ran into USAAF Spitfires. The Focke-Wulfs had to release their bombs into the sea and escape.

Such frustrations would plague the *Gruppe*. During the afternoon of the 8th, five Fw 190s attempted to attack ships in the Mediterranean east of Hammamet, but the mission was in vain. Later that day, 15 of II./Sch.G. 2's Fw 190s along with seven from III./SKG 10, all led by Dörnbrack, went out to attack ships south of Pantelleria. When they could not be found, the Focke-Wulf pilots once again dropped their bombs into the sea.

Another anti-shipping mission on 11 June proved more successful, although it came too late to save Pantelleria, which had been bombed into submission, with Allied troops landing on the island's shore that morning. Nevertheless, in the afternoon, 25 Fw 190s from II./Sch.G. 2, escorted by Bf 109s from I./JG 53, defied enemy fighters and light, ship-mounted AA fire to bomb vessels in and around Pantelleria Harbour. A 6000-ton transport was claimed sunk and two others hit. Immediately after their attack, the Fw 190s raced away to the northeast to evade the fighters, but one pilot of 5. *Staffel* was shot down into the sea.

Operations continued for the rest of June. A strike by the *Schlachtflieger* against an enemy convoy off Tunisia was planned for the evening of the 20th, but as Generalfeldmarschall von Richthofen, who had arrived in the Mediterranean from the USSR to take command of *Luftflotte* 2, lamented, 'It couldn't be carried out as the *Schlachtverbände* need over 45 minutes to form up because the airfields have been badly damaged by enemy air raids'.

Von Richthofen paid a visit to II./Sch.G. 2 in Sardinia on 26 June, elements of the unit having first arrived there on the 19th. He was not satisfied with what he had observed, and noted that he had been left with the impression the unit was 'worn out and needs a rest. A new airfield must urgently be sought as Alghero is a large, peacetime airfield on the edge of the sea, and it can be attacked at any time'.

On or around 20 June, I./Sch.G. 2 relocated from Brindisi, where it had been training up on the Fw 190, to Milis in central Sardinia. It arrived with around 25 Fw 190A-5s and 12 F-3s. To some extent, II./Sch.G. 2's exit from Sicily had been enabled by the arrival on that island of the *Stab*, II. and IV./SKG 10, which bolstered the Fw 190 attack force with fresh pilots and aircraft. It also meant that Sardinia gained some protection against anticipated Allied operations. To 9 July, things had been relatively quiet for the two *Gruppen*, with the exception of mounting overwater reconnaissance patrols looking for signs of an Allied invasion of either Sicily or Sardinia. This 'calm' was shattered on 10 July when the Allies launched Operation *Husky*, with airborne

Feldwebel Josef Enzensberger of I./Schl.G. 2 with an Fw 190 of either the *Geschwaderstab* Schl.G. 2 or the *Gruppenstab I. Gruppe*, photographed at Brindisi in May 1943 during the *Gruppe's* re-equipping with the Focke-Wulf (*Petrick/Jessen*)

and amphibious landings occurring along the southeastern coast of Sicily between the Gulf of Gela and the Gulf of Augusta.

Not surprisingly, Sch.G. 2 was called back to northern Sicily, operating from Chinisia, from where it quickly carried out three strikes against the American landings involving 27 sorties. On the morning of the 11th, two Fw 190s from Sch.G. 2 flew a reconnaissance mission along the coast between Marsala and Comiso. Upon their return, the pilots were able to provide detailed observations on enemy activity around Gela and other coastal areas.

In the afternoon, aircraft from the unit attacked shipping off the west of Sicily, inflicting a hit on a 3500-ton ship loaded with tanks, as well as three landing craft. American tanks were the target for six Fw 190s that evening near Canicatti and Delia. This, of course, was more in keeping with the tactical modus operandi of the *Schlachtgruppen*, and they flew once again against enemy armour from dawn on 12 July, although their supply of bombs, especially of SC 250s, had run down rapidly. Another attack in the morning against tanks near Naro, southwest of Canicatti, resulted in two being set on fire as a result of strafing. Five Fw 190s, accompanied by four Bf 109s of II./JG 53, returned to the area that afternoon, bombing vehicles and tanks on the road between the two locations. At 1910 hrs, it was the turn of three Bf 109s from II./JG 77 to escort another five Fw 190s from Sch.G. 2 in a raid on vehicles at a crossroads near Naro. This time two bombs were dropped, but results could not be observed.

For all the Luftwaffe's efforts, however, Allied strength proved too great, and on 26 July Hitler agreed reluctantly and tentatively to the evacuation of Sicily. On 3 August, Italian forces began to leave the island across the Messina Straits, followed by German units the next day. By 17 August it was over, and Lt Gen George S Patton, commanding Seventh Army, accepted the Axis surrender in Messina. The next bitter battle into which the *Schlachtflieger* would be committed would be that to defend the Italian mainland – the last stronghold in the Mediterranean.

COLOUR PLATES

1
Fw 190A-5/U3 Wk-Nr 1123 'Red L' of Leutnant Armin Rohnstock, 6./Sch.G 1, Deblin-Irena, Poland, spring 1943

2
Fw 190A-5/U3 'White M' possibly of 5./Sch.G 1, probably Ukraine, March–April 1943

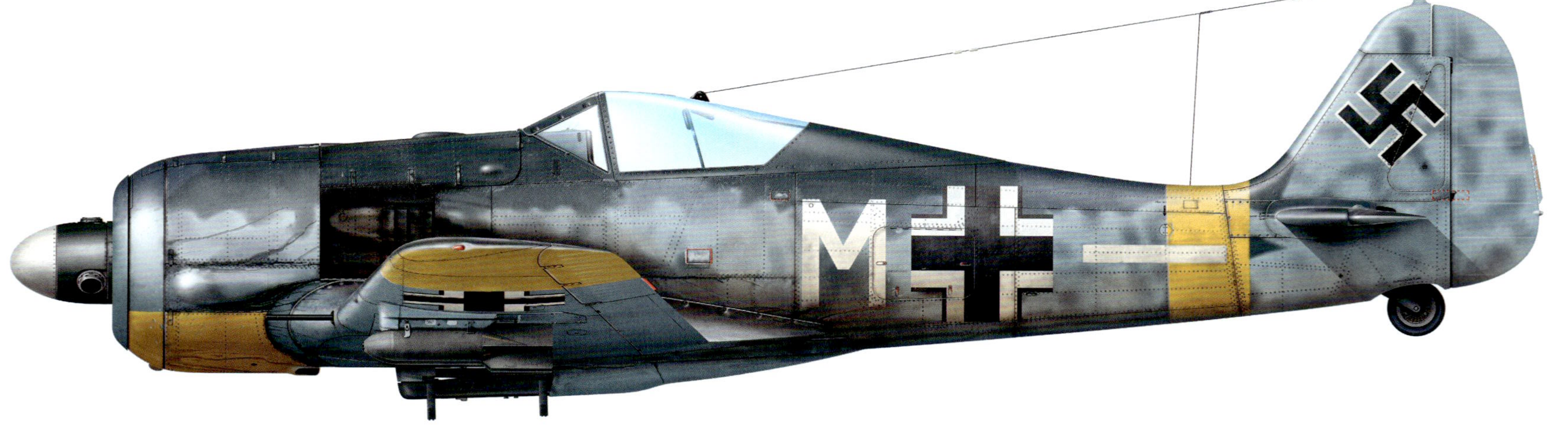

3

Fw 190A-5/U3 'White B' + 'Bar' of 5./Sch.G 2, Sicily, late summer 1943

4

Fw 190A-6 'Black Chevron and T' + 'Bar' of Hauptmann Johannes Meinicke, *Staffelkapitän*, 1./Sch.G 1, Bryansk or Konotop, USSR, August–September 1943

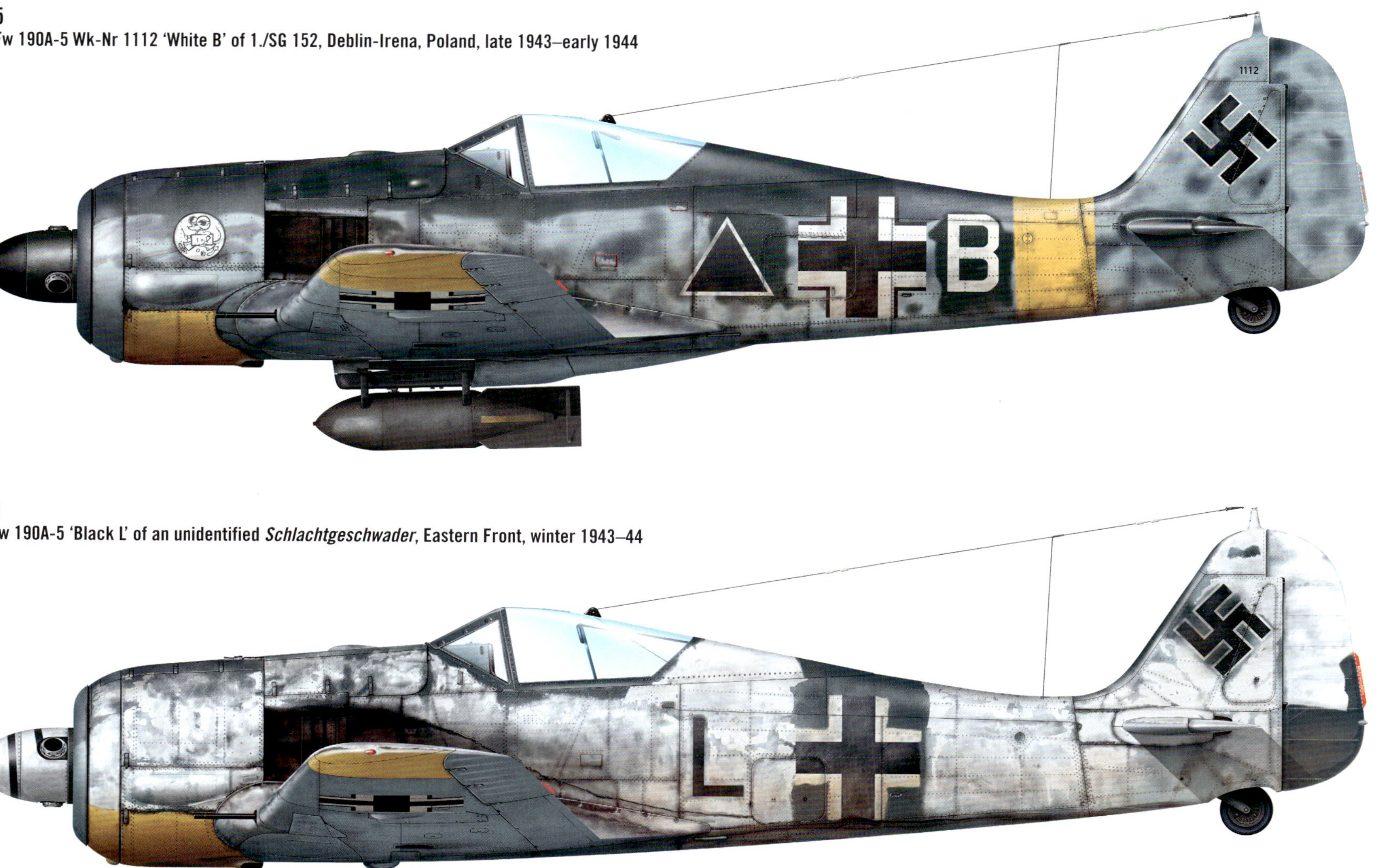

5
Fw 190A-5 Wk-Nr 1112 'White B' of 1./SG 152, Deblin-Irena, Poland, late 1943–early 1944

6
Fw 190A-5 'Black L' of an unidentified *Schlachtgeschwader*, Eastern Front, winter 1943–44

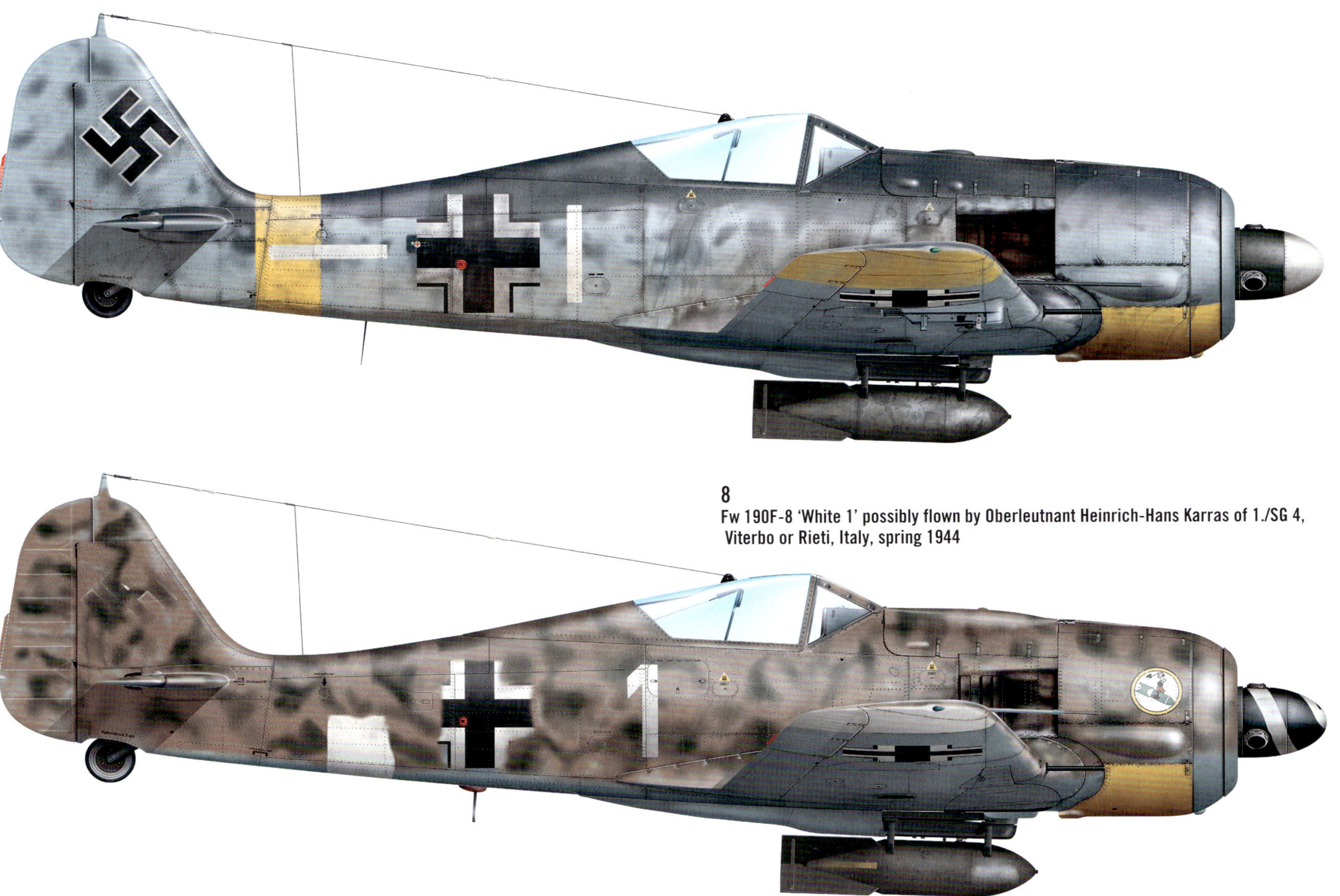

7
Fw 190F-3 'White I' + 'Bar' of 4./SG 3, East Prussia, winter 1943–44

8
Fw 190F-8 'White 1' possibly flown by Oberleutnant Heinrich-Hans Karras of 1./SG 4, Viterbo or Rieti, Italy, spring 1944

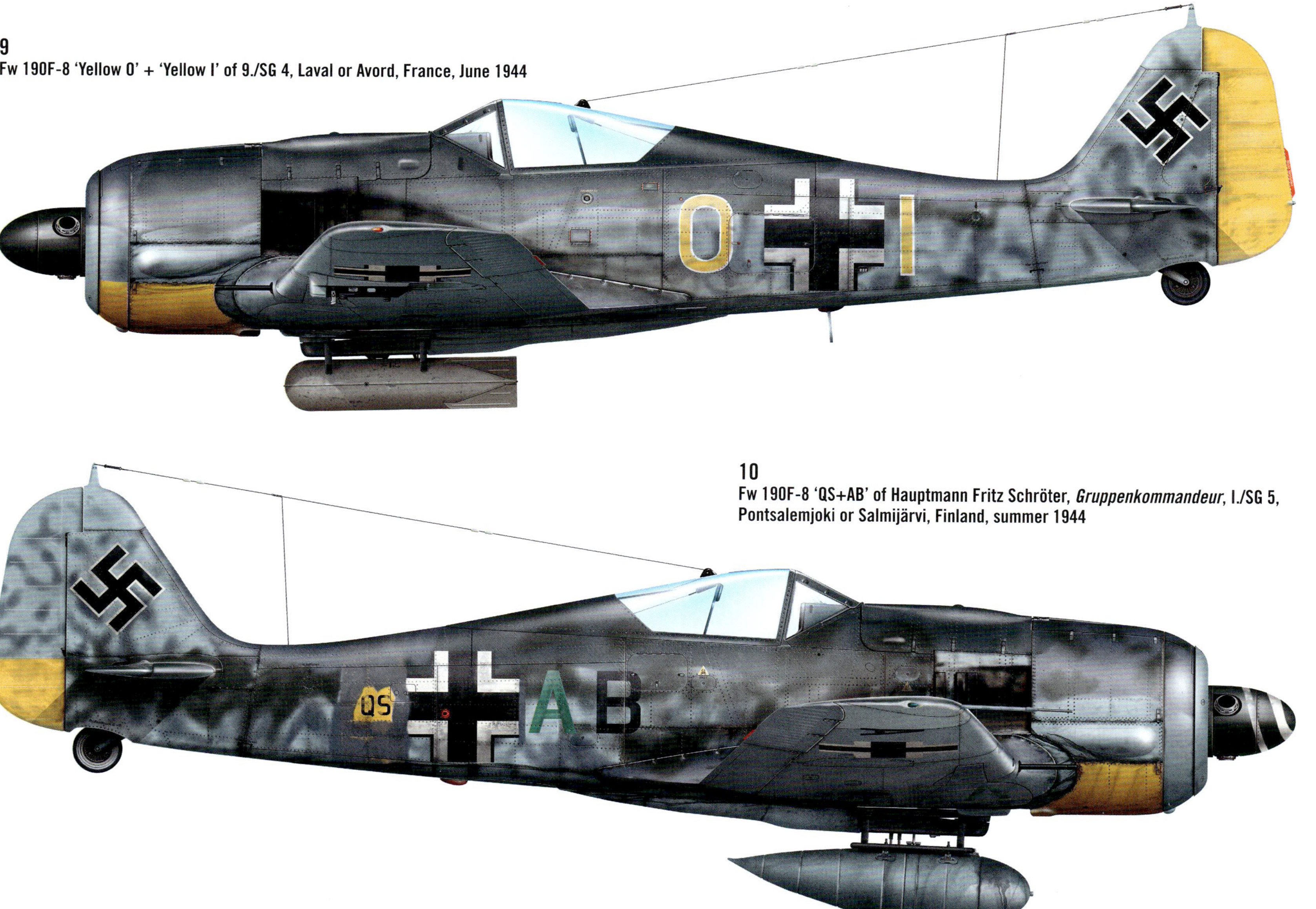

9
Fw 190F-8 'Yellow 0' + 'Yellow I' of 9./SG 4, Laval or Avord, France, June 1944

10
Fw 190F-8 'QS+AB' of Hauptmann Fritz Schröter, *Gruppenkommandeur*, I./SG 5, Pontsalemjoki or Salmijärvi, Finland, summer 1944

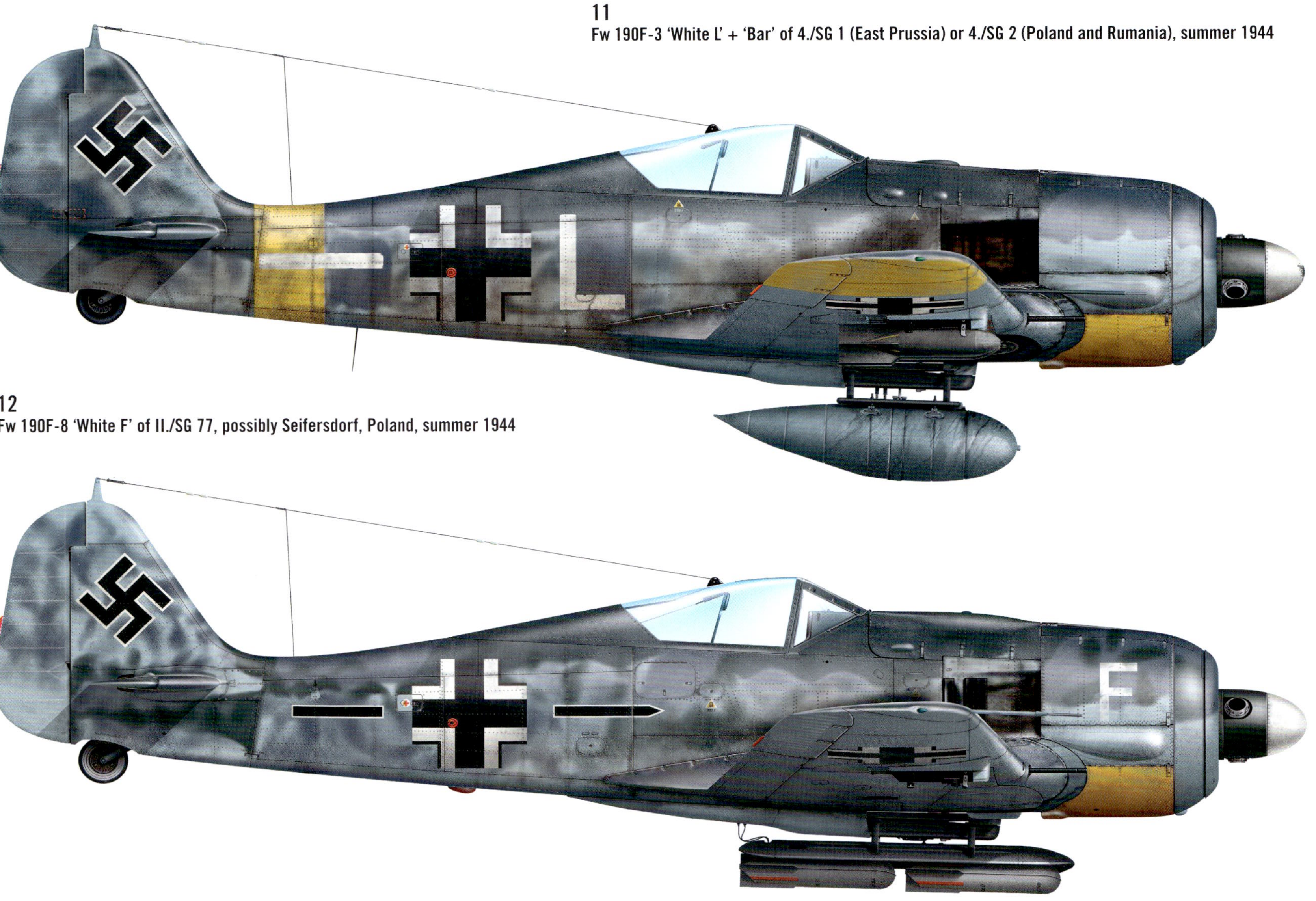

11
Fw 190F-3 'White L' + 'Bar' of 4./SG 1 (East Prussia) or 4./SG 2 (Poland and Rumania), summer 1944

12
Fw 190F-8 'White F' of II./SG 77, possibly Seifersdorf, Poland, summer 1944

13
Fw 190A-4 'BK+WV' and 'White 24' of 1./SG 101, Reims, France, February 1943–April 1944, or Wischau, Czechoslovakia, April 1944–February 1945

14
Fw 190F-8 of I./SG 10, Udetfeld, Germany, December 1944

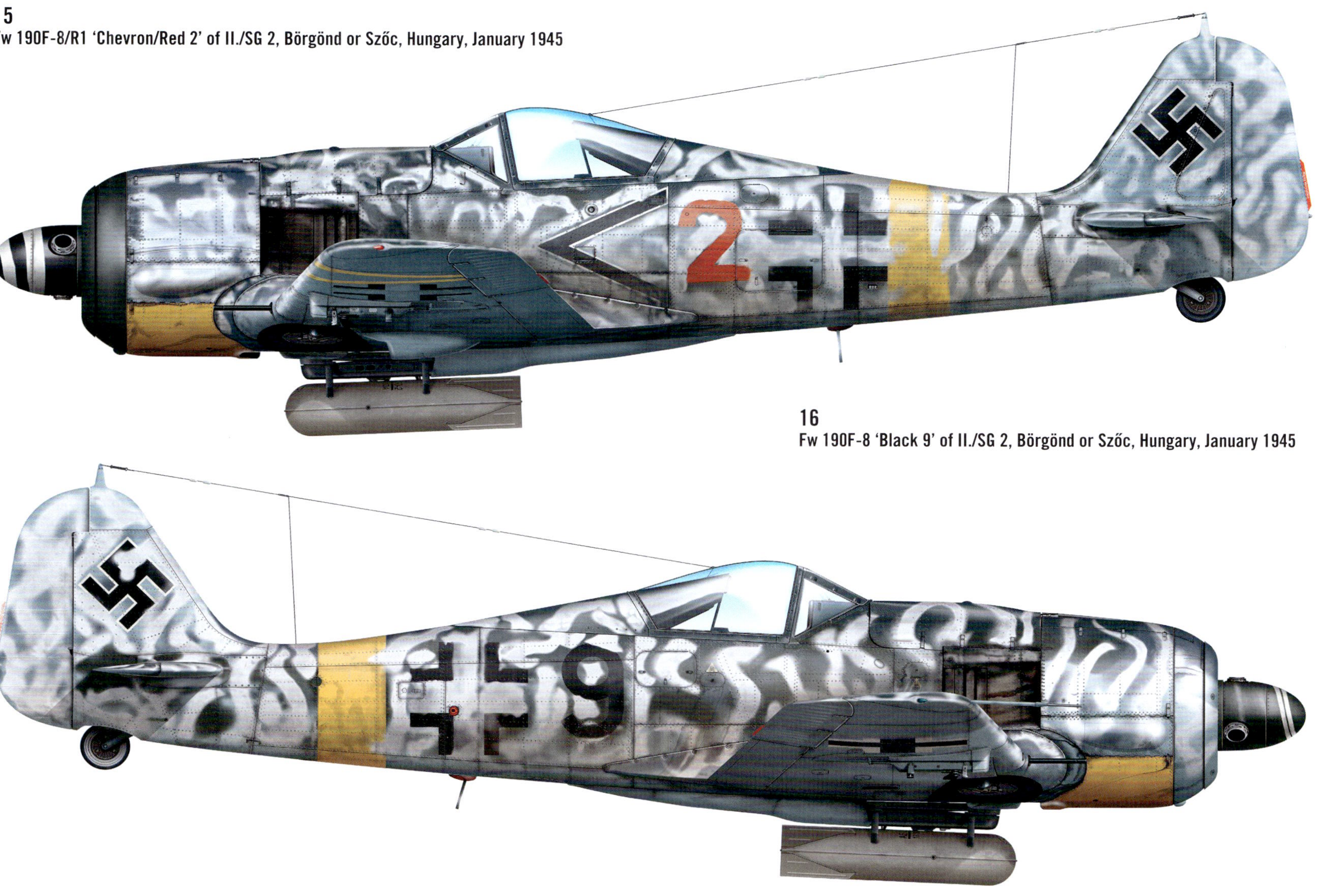

15
Fw 190F-8/R1 'Chevron/Red 2' of II./SG 2, Börgönd or Szőc, Hungary, January 1945

16
Fw 190F-8 'Black 9' of II./SG 2, Börgönd or Szőc, Hungary, January 1945

17
Fw 190F-8/R1 Wk Nr 588717 'Chevron'/Green 3' + 'Bar' of *Stab* II./SG 2, Milovice, Protectorate of Bohemia and Moravia, early 1945

18
Fw 190F-8 'Chevron/Yellow K' of SG 10, Ceské Budejovice, Protectorate of Bohemia and Moravia, April 1945

19
Fw 190F-8/R1 'Black 3' + 'Bar' of *Geschwaderstab*/SG 10, Ceské Budejovice, Protectorate of Bohemia and Moravia, April 1945

20
Fw 190F-8/R1 'Black 6' + 'Bar' and 'White 70' of *Geschwaderstab*/SG 10, Ceské Budejovice, Protectorate of Bohemia and Moravia, April 1945

CHAPTER FIVE

THE EAST – 1943–44

The pilots of a pair of Fw 190F-3s of 5./Schl.G. 1 wait at cockpit readiness on an airstrip in the southern Soviet Union. The wheel doors of the aircraft have been removed so as to prevent earth and debris found on the rough surfaces of forward landing grounds from being caught between the doors and the mainwheels (*EN Archive*)

From a Luftwaffe perspective, the air war on the Eastern Front was fought predominantly and necessarily against the Red Army and not the Soviet Air Force. The massed armoured formations and infantry divisions had to be stopped and neutralised. In fundamental terms, this resulted in the Luftwaffe deploying the bulk of its ground-attack units in the East and, by comparison, the minimum necessary in the West. This is illustrated by the fact that on 25 May 1944, of the 278 aircraft on the strength of VIII. *Fliegerkorps* headquartered in Poland, no fewer than 203 comprised the Fw 190s, Ju 87s and Hs 129s making up SGs 9, 10 and 77.

Yet the delivery of Focke-Wulfs to the recently redesignated Fw 190-equipped *Schlachtgruppen* based on the Eastern Front in the first half of 1944 was frustratingly slow. This was attributable largely to shortfalls in aircraft production as a result of Allied bombing of the Reich's factories, and the necessary priority for the building of Fw 190 *fighters* to protect those centres of production from attack. In January 1944, as the Red Army broke the German grip around Leningrad in the north, then launched a new offensive aimed at encircling Wehrmacht forces in the Cherkassy salient in Ukraine, there were just four *Gruppen* of Fw 190s operational on a front that spanned from Lake Ladoga in the north to the Crimea in the south. These units were all based in the south.

The only *Geschwader* to be fully equipped with the Fw 190 as a *Schlacht* aircraft at this time was SG 10 under Oberstleutnant Helmut Viedebantt, a former SKG 10 pilot and holder of the Knight's Cross. The unit had been based initially at Berditschew, in northern Ukraine, 40 km south of Zhitomir, before moving to Nikolayev. I./SG 10, under Major Egon Thiem, a veteran of II.(*Schlacht*)/LG 2 who been awarded the Knight's Cross in July 1940, and II./SG 10, under Major Götz Baumann, followed Viedebantt's *Stab* from Berditschew to Nikolayev, where they flew operations in support of Army Group A against the 3rd Ukrainian Front. III./SG 10, led by the Stuka veteran and Knight's Cross recipient Major Helmut Leicht, had recently formed up and was at Lysiatycze, in southern Poland.

Operating a mix of F-3s and G-3s, SG 10 would be employed in intensive operations through to the spring, and would suffer very heavy losses in both aircraft and pilots.

II./SG 77, whose command was in transition from Hauptmann Siegfried Steinhoff to Hauptmann Alexander Gläser, was at Kalinovka, where it too was deployed in the Zhitomir area with Fw 190F-2/3s.

Elsewhere, II./SG 2, under Hauptmann Werner Dörnbrack, was at Bagerovo in the eastern Crimea with A-4s, A-5s and F-3s, where it was engaged in attacking Soviet transport routes and airfields on the Taman Peninsula, as well as striking artillery batteries in the Syvash area, just to the north of the Crimea.

Typical of the young *Schlachtflieger* serving on the Eastern Front from mid-1943 was 23-year-old Rhinelander Leutnant Fritz Seyffardt, who was posted to II./Schl.G. 1 (II./SG 2 from October 1943) in the Crimea, led at the time by Knight's Cross holder Hauptmann Heinz Frank. Seyffardt had undergone his operational training in early 1943 with the specialist ground-attack training wing SG 101, followed by a spell at the *Ergänzungs-Zerstörergruppe* at Deblin-Irena, where he instructed on Bf 109s and Hs 123s.

At the time of Seyffardt's arrival with II./Schl.G. 1, the unit retained some of its old Hs 123s alongside the Fw 190s with which it had re-equipped from January 1943. Seyffardt recalled;

'In 1942 I saw and flew my first Fw 190. I was thrilled with this machine. The Bf 109 didn't appeal to me because it was dangerous in dives (wing failure), and on take-off and landing because of its narrow landing gear.

'The difference between the Fw 190 and the Bf 109 was that there was more room in the Focke-Wulf's cockpit and the controls were simpler – for example, landing flaps and trim were electric. Another pronounced difference was the stability of the Fw 190. Thanks to its through-wing spars and wide landing gear, the machine was substantially more stable and robust in flight, and especially in landing on rough fields. Visibility was better in flight than with the Bf 109, although worse on take-off and

Three Fw 190s (the canopy of the third Focke-Wulf is just visible at far right) of an unidentified *Schlacht* unit, with crudely applied winter 'camouflage', prepare to take off from a snow-coated airfield in the Soviet Union. As the aircraft carry no offensive load, it is possible this was the start of a transfer flight (*EN Archive*)

landing because of the Focke-Wulf's three-point attitude. At great height, engine performance was inadequate. Otherwise, the machine was pleasant to fly and, for the most part, had no critical or dangerous characteristics.

'Normal range for our F-models was approximately 600–700 km. The average mission on the Russian Front lasted 45–60 minutes. Firepower was very good. As a rule, we had two 20 mm cannon and two machine guns. There was also provision for the installation of an additional two 20 mm cannon in the outer wing panels.

'I joined II./Schl.G. 1 in 1943 at Anapa, on the Black Sea. From there we moved to a grass field at Varvarovka, southwest of Kharkov, which became our base for the great Kursk offensive. In the following months we remained in the southern sector, flying from various fields behind the frontlines. Later, we participated in operations over Sevastopol until the end of the fighting there. I flew around 500 frontline missions and had to make several belly landings on differing terrain – something that could be done without undue difficulty. Once, I had to bail out right over Sevastopol, as my machine had been shot down in flames. The radial engine was subject to improper cooling of the rear cylinders, resulting in engine failures and belly landings.

'As a *Schlachtflieger*, I had less to do with enemy fighters than with enemy ground-attack machines, of which I shot down 30. We also had contact with Russian fighters, but for the most part they avoided us, so we had no real problem with them.

'As a flying tactic, we had the greatest success when we flew "open" – in other words, approximately 80–100 m separation from aircraft to aircraft. In the target area, we split into the small, two-aircraft *Rotte* elements for the attack, only reassembling into larger formations on the return flight.'

Seyffardt flew with 5./SG 2 until 15 June 1944, when he was posted to 1./SG 152 at Prossnitz as an Fw 190 *Schlachtflugzeug* instructor, eventually becoming the unit's *Staffelkapitän*. He was awarded the Knight's Cross on 8 August 1944 in recognition of 470 missions, although, as he mentions, he would end the war having flown some 500. His remarkable tally of 30 enemy aircraft shot down was, without doubt, impressive for a *Schlacht* pilot, but not unique.

In January 1944, during operations over the Kerch Strait, in addition to carrying out *Schlacht* operations, and in an indication of the Luftwaffe's paucity in fighters, *Luftflotte* 4 ordered II./SG 2 to intercept Soviet aircraft over the area. Hauptmann Karl-Günther Bleckmann of 6. *Staffel*

Fw 190A-5 'White B' of 1./SG 152 at Deblin-Irena or Prossnitz in the spring–summer of 1944. SG 152 was an operational training and replacement unit formed from the *Ergänzungs-Schlachtgruppe*. The aircraft seen here features a variation of the Mickey Mouse emblem favoured by the *Schlacht* units, and it also has the black triangle marking denoting a ground-attack unit, suggesting that this Fw 190A-5 had previously belonged to an operational *Gruppe* (*EN Archive*)

This formal photograph of Oberleutnant Fritz Seyffardt was taken shortly after he had received the Knight's Cross on 8 August 1944, at which time he was *Staffelkapitän* of 5./SG 2. He recalled being 'thrilled' when he first flew the Fw 190. Seyffardt would go on to serve, successively, as *Kapitän* of 10. and 12./SG 151 and 12./SG 2. He flew 506 operational missions, and is credited with 30 aerial victories, all claimed as a *Schlachtflieger* (*EN Archive*)

claimed three P-39s shot down between 26–28 January, while Oberfeldwebel Hans Willmerdinger accounted for an Il-2. By 25 February, 6./SG 2 had claimed 11 enemy fighters shot down, five of these being credited to Bleckmann. He was killed a few months later on 4 June when his Fw 190 caught fire while returning from a mission in Rumania.

Also serving in 5./SG 2 was Leutnant August Lambert, whose record in the USSR was remarkable. His service mirrored that of Seyffardt's in that he had also flown with II./Schl.G. 1, and with whom, as an Oberfeldwebel, he first embarked on operational flying in the southern Soviet Union. In the spring of 1944, while partaking in operations around Sevastopol, he apparently increased his tally of aerial kills from 20 to 90. Indeed, as fellow II./SG 2 pilot Oberfeldwebel Hermann Buchner commented, 'he shot down Russians like flies'.

Lambert's score included instances in which he accounted for several enemy aircraft shot down in a day, such as on 17 April when his accomplishments earned him a mention in the daily Wehrmacht communique. 'Leutnant Lambert alone destroyed 12 enemy aircraft'. He accounted for nine more on 4 May and 14 two days later. On another day, Lambert was credited with no fewer than 17 enemy aircraft shot down. These were figures which many of the Luftwaffe's fighter aces could envy. On 14 May, Lambert was awarded the Knight's Cross, having flown more than 300 missions and accounted for 90 aircraft shot down, as well as scores of tanks, vehicles and guns destroyed in customary *Schlachtflieger* operations.

On 27 April, II./SG 2 earned a mention in the *Oberkommando der Wehrmacht* (Armed Forces High Command) daily reports for its accomplishments over the Crimea in the period 12–16 April, during which time it was credited with destroying 106 enemy aircraft in the air and a further 28 on the ground.

But Soviet fighters were no 'easy meat'. From September 1943 to the end of the war, Feldwebel Peter Traubel flew Fw 190Fs with II./SG 2 and later SG 4 in the East. Although he appreciated the flying qualities of the Focke-Wulf, he was also aware of the dangers;

'I had the chance to inspect a Soviet fighter once that had bellied in. Those Russian aircraft were primitively equipped, but in the air were an enemy to be taken seriously. In turns, they were the equal of an Fw 190, if not even more manoeuvrable. When they appeared, we'd drop our external loads, as otherwise we could have been sitting ducks for the Russians.

'During combat, we feared the great risk of fire from being hit. I remember that a fellow pilot burned in his cockpit when he was hit in the fuel system. The inside of his aircraft instantly burst into flames. Even without enemy aircraft, there was a dangerous enemy to be feared. That was the ground defences. I recall a day when four of us flew an attack against an enemy supply column. All three of my comrades were brought down by enemy Flak. We never learned their fates.'

Progress through expansion remained slow, and by late spring 1944 only 4./SG 5 – formed at Petsamo, in Finland, by absorbing a small number of Fw 190A-2s and A-3s of 14.(*Jabo*)/JG 5 – and III./SG 1 at Wilna and Radzyn had been activated beyond the *Gruppen* of SG 10 and II./SG 77.

Between March and May 1944, a concern hung over SG 10's presence in the USSR. The Nazi leadership harboured fears over Allied intentions to occupy neutral Turkish territory either with the consent or support of Turkey, or even against its will, for the purpose of executing air warfare against the Balkans or for moving northwards against Bulgaria from any secured Turkish territory.

In such an instance, at the issuing of the codeword '*Gertrud*', the whole of SG 10, along with *Stab*, I. and II./SG 4 (see Chapter Six) and other bomber and fighter *Gruppen*, was to move to Bulgaria as part of *Luftwaffenkommando Süd-Ost* under the jurisdiction of 1. *Fliegerdivision*, with the *Stab*, I. and III. *Gruppen* going to Okop and II./SG 10 to Jasbul. Fw 190s would be expected to operate over enemy landing areas and any ports, bridges, airfields and communication centres taken by enemy forces. Fortunately for the Germans, this contingency was never needed.

By June, of 19 *Schlachtgruppen* formed (excluding the Hs 129-equipped SG 9), only half were fully equipped with Fw 190F/Gs, with the remainder continuing to operate the Ju 87. It was forecast that I./SG 5's conversion would be complete by 15 July, II./SG 1 on 10 July, I./SG 77 on 20 July and I. and II./SG 3 by the end of July or early August. Gradually, over the coming weeks, more Focke-Wulfs were delivered, and by August, in addition to SG 10, Fw 190s increasingly arrived with the *Gruppen* of SGs 1, 2, 3, 5 and 77.

To the north, in Finland, 1./SG 5 under Oberleutnant Franz-Josef Schoppe was assigned to a specially formed composite 'battle group', *Gefechtsverband Kuhlmey*. Led by Stuka ace Oberstleutnant Kurt Kuhlmey, the *Gefechtsverband* had arrived at Immola on 16 June with 23 Ju 87D-5s and 23 Fw 190A-6s and F-8s of I./SG 3 and 1./SG 5, respectively. These were soon supplemented by the Fw 190 fighters of II./JG 54 and a small number of Bf 109 reconnaissance aircraft. It had also been intended to send III./SG 3 if it had completed conversion to the Fw 190, but the earliest the *Gruppe* was expected to be ready was 1 July.

An Fw 190, believed to be the aircraft of Oberleutnant Franz-Josef Schoppe, *Staffelkapitän* of 1./SG 5, is bombed up at Immola, Finland, in July 1944. A 500-kg bomb has been raised up to the aircraft's ETC 501 rack using a hydraulic LWC 500 hydraulic bomb trolley. The aircraft retains the emblem of 14.(*Jabo*)/JG 5, that *Staffel* having been redesignated 4./SG 5 in February 1944. 4./SG 5 was redesignated again as a new 1./SG 5 on 17 May, when the original 1. *Staffel* became 2./NSGr. 8 equipped with Ju 87s. All these units were based, variously, in Finland and Norway (*Robert Forsyth Collection*)

The task of the *Gefechtsverband* was to render support to Finnish forces resisting the strong Soviet offensive which had broken through the Finnish Mannerheim Line.

For their first few days in Finland, sensibly, Schoppe's *Schlachtflieger* had conducted flights to familiarise themselves with the local terrain, weather and enemy positions, but in the process had lost four Fw 190F-8s – at least two of these were attributed to engine failure. On 23 June, albeit understrength, 1./SG 5 went into action, flying 23 sorties on that day alone against the vital road and rail bridges at Tali. From then on, a mini campaign was waged between Red Army engineers endeavouring to repair the bridges and the Stuka crews and *Schlachtflieger* flying repeat missions to destroy them, the Fw 190s dropping 250- and 500-kg bombs.

Meanwhile, at a command meeting on 20 June, Göring asked that the move of the rest of I./SG 5 to *Gefechtsverband Kuhlmey* be 'accelerated'.

Operations took their toll, and despite *Luftflotte* 5 establishing an efficient resupply line, on 26 June there were only four operational Fw 190F-8s. Two days later, evidently having seen an improvement in serviceability, under escort from II./JG 54, 1./SG 5 flew 30 sorties, dropping 69 tons of bombs. Such operations prevented Soviet forces from penetrating the line at Tali–Ihantala. The Soviet Air Force responded by attacking *Gefechtsverband Kuhlmey*'s aircraft at Immola, destroying four Ju 87s and six Fw 190s in one of the hangars there. 1./SG 5 eventually responded on 31 July with an attack on Heinjoki airfield in which nine Soviet aircraft were destroyed.

SG 5 numbered only one complete *Gruppe* – I. *Gruppe*, which had been deployed in Finland and over the northern Soviet Union since October. Based at Pori, in southern Finland, it had commenced conversion to the Fw 190 from the Ju 87 in early June 1944. This process was completed by late July with the arrival of 30 F-8s, and by which time the unit was under the command of Hauptmann Fritz Schröter, the former *Kommandeur* of III./SKG 10. The *Gruppe* then moved to Pöntiönjoki.

On 3 August, 20 Fw 190s of I./SG 5 were transferred to Utti, including those of 1. *Staffel* which been assigned to *Gefechtsverband Kuhlmey*, for operations against Soviet shipping in the Gulf of Finland. The Focke-Wulfs remaining at Immola carried out several strikes against the enemy bridgehead at Kivijäri in Äyräpää, while on 5 August the *Staffel* lost Unteroffizier Gössl when his Fw 190 was hit by AA fire during an attack on artillery batteries in the Ihantala–Portinhoikka area. On the 7th, a force of 21 Fw 190F-8s attacked the Soviet airfield at Lavansaari, and the following day 20 Focke-Wulfs again struck at shipping.

I./SG 5's time at Utti would not last long, however, with the *Gruppe* relocating to Estonia shortly thereafter. Between 7 July and 8 August, 1. *Staffel* had had two pilots wounded and two Fw 190s destroyed and four damaged.

Over Estonia during the evening of 14 August, Fw 190s from Hauptmann Erwin-Peter Diekwisch's 3./SG 5 conducted an attack in the Röuge area. Flying in a *Schwarm* of F-8s on that mission was one of the 'senior' pilots in the *Staffel*, Oberfeldwebel Gotthard Roediger. He would claim his first aerial victory during the sortie, as he later reported;

'After the bombing of the village of Linnamde at 1920 hrs, I spotted a Russian fighter at an altitude of about 600 m and, while moving into attack position at about 50 m below it, I saw a formation of five Il-2s flying over

Röuge on a westerly course. From my greater altitude, I went to attack at high speed and noticed hits in one of the aircraft, which then left the formation in a left turn, trailing smoke. Due to my high speed and the return fire from the rear gunner, I was unable to observe what happened to the aircraft any further.'

Roediger's attack was witnessed by his *Staffelkamerad*, Leutnant Viktor von Stryck;

'At about 1920 hrs, after bombs had been dropped, I noticed five Il-2s to the left and below us in the Röuge area, which we attacked with our onboard armament. Oberfeldwebel Roediger scored hits on the second aircraft to the left. The aircraft sheared away steeply downwards and emitted a lot of smoke. I was unable to observe the impact as we had overtaken the *Schwarm* in the meantime.'

Roediger would be fortunate in as much as the following day Hauptmann Schröter flew over the same area and noticed the wreckage of an Il-2 that had hit the ground there. Roediger became another *Schlachtflieger* to claim an aerial victory. And yet, as former II./SG 2 pilot Oberfeldwebel Hermann Buchner recounted, despite winning accolades for their prowess as 'fighter pilots', 'In *Schlachter* circles there was still an aversion to aerial fighting. According to instructions, our principal task was to engage in combat against ground targets. But there were still a few members of the old "Schl.G. 1" *Gruppe* remaining who had fighter pilot blood running through their veins. But to be a good fighter pilot, you have to be born that way'.

In this regard, in late June 1944, while based in Rumania, Buchner discussed the subject of Fw 190s being 'necessarily' used as fighters with the *Kommandeur* of II./SG 2, Hauptmann Dörnbrack. It seems Dörnbrack did not relish this development, and shortly after the *Gruppe* relocated to a base on the Trotus River the emphasis returned to ground-attack operations. This cheered Buchner, who, by July, had flown more missions than any other pilot in II./SG 2;

'Again we flew operations against Russian positions and troop concentrations – proper *Schlachtflieger* stuff. Slowly, the young pilots of

Oberstleutnant Alfred Druschel, the *Inspizient der Tag-Schlachtfliegerverbände beim General der Schlachtflieger*, shakes hands with Oberfeldwebel Hermann Buchner (centre) at Prossnitz after presenting the latter with the Knight's Cross on 30 July 1944. Buchner had not long returned from the Eastern Front, where he had been *Staffelkapitän* of 4./SG 2. He had been transferred out of the frontline to take over a *Staffel* in the operational training *Gruppe*, I./SG 152. Buchner is seen here alongside Major Heinz Frank, holder of the Knight's Cross and Oak Leaves and formerly of II./SG 2. He would take command of IV./SG 151 shortly after this photograph was taken. Photograph via Hermann Buchner (*Robert Forsyth Collection*)

4. *Staffel* learned to fight, they became tougher and even took the fight to the Russians. They learned to fly and learned to value the Fw 190. It was a joy to see how they developed, how they stayed with the *Gruppe* in formation during operations.'

From the summer of 1944, as the war in the East became one of defence for the Germans, so the vast, open battlefields proved favourable to ground-attack units, especially in the destruction of enemy armour. Generalmajor Hitschhold told his Allied captors that he believed the *Schlachtgruppen* could have halted the final Soviet offensive against Germany from mid-1944 had they had enough fuel to fly more missions. Indeed, such was the faith in the *Schlacht* units' capabilities against enemy tanks that Generaloberst Heinz Guderian, the Inspector General of the Panzer Troops and the last Chief of the Army General Staff, was instrumental in securing allocations of fuel specifically for their use.

Some of the more successful *Schlacht* pilots notched up extraordinarily high mission tallies in the Fw 190 over the Eastern Front. One of the most impressive in this regard was Leutnant Kurt Plenzat, a Prussian who flew with 2./StG 2 (2./SG 2) for the duration of the war, seeing service on the Channel Front, in the Balkans and over Crete before his unit was sent East. Here, he took part in operations from Leningrad, to Demyansk, Stalingrad, Kursk, Kharkov and the Crimea.

Plenzat was awarded the Knight's Cross on 19 September 1943 for 652 missions as a Ju 87 pilot, and he survived being shot down on several occasions. When II./SG 2 converted to the Fw 190 in the autumn of that year, he went on to fly around 600 missions in the Focke-Wulf as a *Schlacht* pilot, during the course of which he destroyed many tanks and shot down a Soviet aircraft.

Oberleutnant Manfred Goetze was appointed *Staffelkapitän* of 8./SG 10 on 24 February 1944 after the *Staffel* was redesignated from 5./StG 77. Goetze had flown the Ju 87 over the Balkans, Crete and the Soviet Union, distinguishing himself over the central and southern sectors of the Eastern Front. After converting to the Fw 190, he flew hundreds of ground-attack missions over southeast Europe and was also credited with downing eight enemy aircraft.

After operational service flying Ju 87s with StG 3 over the Mediterranean and North Africa, during which he partook in several notable anti-shipping sorties and survived being shot down by American fighters in Tunisia, Leutnant Hubert Pölz moved to the USSR with III./StG 3 in July 1943 and saw action over the central and southern sectors of the Front, including Kharkov, Kiev, the Crimea (where he sank several Soviet vessels) and the Kuban bridgehead. Pölz was appointed *Staffelkapitän* of 7./StG 3 on 28 September 1943 shortly before the unit was redesignated 7./SG 3. From then on he flew the Fw 190 as proficiently as he had flown the Ju 87. Of an eventual total of 1055 missions flown by him, 351 were in the Fw 190, which he used to claim 11 aerial victories.

While in British captivity in October 1945, Major iG Eberhard Jacob wrote a detailed report for his captors explaining how ground-attack missions using Fw 190s were planned and executed during 1944–45. Jacob, a Prussian, was more than qualified for the task. As a young officer cadet, he had attended a course at the *Luftkriegschule* (Air War Academy) at Wildpark-Werder near Berlin, before going on to enjoy an illustrious career as a Stuka pilot, serving in Poland, the West, over England, the Mediterranean and in the USSR, eventually being appointed as *Staffelkapitän* of 4./StG 2 and 7./StG 3. But his superiors decided to cut his operational career short so that his experiences could be used in a run of staff roles with II. *Fliegerkorps*, *Fliegerführer Afrika* and *Luftflotte* 2.

After a brief return to flying duties as *Kommandeur* of III./StG 3 in the Soviet Union in the second half of 1943, Jacob was assigned to Kupfer's *General der Schlachtflieger* staff based at the RLM in Berlin on 5 October, just as the *Schlachtgeschwadern* were being reorganised and redesignated and the Fw 190 was foreseen as becoming the Luftwaffe's prime *Schlacht* aircraft.

According to Jacob, in order for Fw 190 *Schlacht* missions to be executed effectively, it was essential that at *Gruppe*-level the unit operations room be located as near as possible to the unit's airfield so as to be able to overlook both it and the dispersal areas in order to be able to supervise take-offs and landings. However, in an environment of enemy air superiority, or where there were frequent enemy strafing attacks, this was not possible.

Jacob also stressed the importance of a reliable signals infrastructure, including telephone and radio links to the parent *Geschwaderstab* and the *Gruppe*'s component *Staffeln*, as well as to the designated radio beacon and direction finder and *Egon* control stations. In addition, ideally, preferably a physical or, if not, a wire link should exist between the *Gruppe* command post and a unit radio room/station which controlled communications with aircraft in the air and with ground units that the unit was supporting. If no sufficient airfield signals infrastructure was available, then a Ju 52/3m transport fitted with mobile radio equipment should be provided by the area *Luftflotte* or *Fliegerkorps*.

Three key officers in the *Gruppenstab* were the Intelligence Officer, whose contribution, as described by Jacob, 'lay in a painfully exact keeping of the enemy situation and in the receiving and immediate evaluation of the most minor reconnaissance reports'; the Operations Officer, whose main task was maintaining the latest situation map as it pertained to friendly forces, and who 'strived especially hard to keep up with the latest developments in the locations of the frontlines'; and the Meteorological Officer. In respect to the job performed by the latter officer, Jacob noted;

'For ground-attack units, the *local* weather situation and the short-range prediction were of special interest. The larger weather picture and long-range predictions were unimportant. Since the facts needed for ground-attack missions could usually be supplied by the airfield meteorologists or from superior units, the meteorologist on the *Geschwaderstab* was superfluous.'

As many as ten Fw 190s of an unidentified *Schlachtgruppe* can be seen here amidst typically bleak operating conditions on the Eastern Front in the winter of 1943–44. Some of the aircraft have been loaded with bombs, suggesting a state of readiness. The Focke-Wulf in the right foreground carries the chevron fuselage marking of a *Stab* aircraft, and it is fitted with dust filters for tropical service and operations from forward airstrips (*EN Archive*)

Whenever possible, a preliminary readiness order for a mission was issued (for example at 20–30 minutes or one hour), but in instances of short notice, the *Staffelkapitäne* would be present in the Operations Room. Mission orders would then be given by the *Gruppenkommandeur* to the *Staffelkapitäne* using maps. The briefing would include information on the latest friendly and enemy ground and air situations and intentions, objective(s) of the mission, details of bomb-loads and fuses, take-off sequence, assembly process, flight formation, route, altitude and points at which frontlines would be crossed.

The time and duration of the attack would also be briefed, as would the type of attack (dive, shallow dive, low-level, bombing and/or strafing), assignment of targets (including which pilots would suppress enemy AA fire and/or take over as 'fighter escort' if none was available) and return flight (assembly, route and altitude). Finally, details pertaining to radio callsigns, conduct and cooperation with friendly ground forces, fighter escort – if available (rendezvous and formation) – navigation, weather and the naming of the deputy flight commander were also given.

The *Staffelkapitäne* would then leave the Operations Room to brief their pilots at their dispersal areas. At this briefing, the *Staffelkapitän* would advise the time to start engines, the sequence for taxiing and the composition of the two-aircraft *Rotten* and four-aircraft *Schwärme*. According to Jacob, 'The *speed* as well as the *exactness* of the dissemination of orders was critical. Since the *Staffelkapitäne* were already in the Operations Room when the mission order arrived, and could be informed immediately, the time required to prepare for take-off (including the briefing of *Staffelkapitäne*, ride of *Staffelkapitäne* from the Operations Room to *Staffel* dispersal areas, briefing of readied crews by the *Staffelkapitäne*, transit of pilots to aircraft, starting up and taxiing to take-off) was not usually more than 15–25 minutes.'

At take-off, every effort was made to avoid 'traffic jams', since the massing of aircraft on an airfield presented a good target for enemy air attacks, and also because the lubrication and cooling of the Fw 190's BMW 801 engine was inefficient at low RPM. As far as was practical, the Fw 190s would taxi in *Rotten* from dispersal and take off as quickly as possible. 'Uninterrupted take-off of one *Rotte* after another was a prerequisite for quick assembly in the air', Jacob wrote, 'The quicker the formation assembled, the less vulnerable it was to enemy attack'.

In the air, the Fw 190 *Schlachtgruppen* would usually adopt a 'Vic' formation, and within each *Schwarm* the lateral spacing between aircraft was five to six wingspans, while they flew at half-an-aircraft length front to rear, and a similar height vertically. The rearmost *Schwarm* in each *Staffel* was stepped up around 45–90 m, and assumed 'fighter cover' if necessary. The *Schwarmführer* would observe the situation on the ground and monitor navigation and route, while the pilots on each flank – often the especially good pilots – would keep a look out for enemy fighters.

The *Gruppe* 'Vic' would be led by the *Stabschwarm*, which included the mission commander, with, in the direction of flight, 1. *Staffel* to port and slightly behind and higher, 2. *Staffel* to starboard and slightly higher and behind, while 3. *Staffel* was at the rear and some 180–360 m higher than the rest of the formation.

When making a dive attack with bombs, *Staffeln* would form up into loose, linear *Gefechtsreihe* ('battle columns') – a formation which, according to Jacob, was 'purposely vague to allow plenty of jockeying around to get on the target and to present no regular target to AA fire. Each *Schwarm* leader stays ahead of his *Schwarm*, but otherwise position goes by the board. The *Rotten* try to keep contact too'.

From 1944, Soviet AA fire became an 'occupational hazard' for the '*Schlachter*'. Hermann Buchner of 6./SG 2 recalled flying a mission from Bagerovo, on the Kerch Peninsula, during the fighting in Crimea;

'On 26 January I was shot at during a low-level attack on Russian positions and only managed to make it to our own lines with a great deal of effort after my engine quit, after which I made an emergency landing behind our lines. I set my machine down in a field northwest of Kerch and it creaked and threw up dust, the tail finally turning through 180 degrees before coming to a stop. However, I had got the aircraft down, and so I crawled from the wreckage – even uninjured!'

Buchner had been lucky, but another valuable Fw 190 had fallen victim to enemy ground fire.

Tactical directives issued in May 1944 stipulated that the direction of the dive during an Fw 190 attack was determined by the wind and the type of target. Attacks would be carried out in the shortest possible time. Cloud or sun cover was utilised if possible, and in such a way that directly after bombs were released – usually from about 900 m – pull-out and the exit flight home would take place over undefended territory. If the attack was to be carried out in a single dive, then bombs would be dropped in salvo or one after the other, depending on the target.

Shallow dive attacks were carried out when the permissible altitude was not sufficient for a dive attack because of ceiling, visibility, or when the target was known to have only weak defence. The dive usually began from 900–1800 m at an angle of 50 to 20 degrees. The attack formation and direction of attack were determined in the same way as a dive attack.

Release height was determined by the types of bombs and fuses used, but ordnance was dropped from as low a height as possible to ensure a greater chance of hits. Depending on the strength of the ground defences and ordnance load, attacks were repeated several times. In such cases, bombs were dropped by aircraft in pairs or singly.

Obviously, when making shallow dive attacks, it was possible to carry out strafing runs as well, and in such instances fire was not opened at more than 750 m from the target. Pilots would aim a little below the target on the run in, and if strikes could be seen on the ground, after the necessary lateral correction, the aircraft was then close enough to ensure that its pilot would strike successfully.

Low-level bombing attacks were mounted by Fw 190s in bad weather or where surprise was required. However, success proved hard to come by with bombs in such attacks, as the weapons had to be dropped with some delayed action in order not to endanger the carrier aircraft. If possible, the pilot would pull up to 275–370 m just before the target in order to aid target recognition and thus, hopefully, carry out a more effective strike. However, given the relatively poor impact of such attacks, low-level

Two Fw 190F-8s of II./SG 77 undergo maintenance at an unidentified airfield. The *Gruppe* was formed on 18 October 1943 as part of the reorganisation of the ground-attack arm and initially placed under the command of Hauptmann Siegfried Steinhoff. Both of these aircraft are fitted with centreline and underwing bomb racks (*EN Archive*)

strafing runs were favoured. These attacks required some preparation, since locating appropriate targets was often difficult.

This was, in principle and theory, how the *Schlachtgeschwadern* went about their operations in the East in 1944.

As a measure of how intense air operations had become for I./SG 10 by the autumn of 1944, in Hungary in the 11 days between 7–18 October – a period in which the *Gruppe* operated from Földes and then Sarospatak – it suffered one pilot lightly wounded following a crash-landing on return from a mission, four pilots missing, one injured after bailing out during air combat and another killed in action. Of these, the unfortunate Oberfeldwebel Ernst Selzer of the *Gruppenstab* crashed-landed in his Fw 190F-8 after returning from a mission and the aircraft turned over. Selzer escaped with light injuries and burns, but the following day he went missing while on a transfer flight in a Fieseler Fi 156 Storch which was ferrying him to a hospital for treatment.

From 19 October, the Fw 190s of Hauptmann Alexander Gläser's II./SG 77 were based at Saalau, an airstrip in East Prussia 17.5 km northwest of Insterburg. The surviving logbook of Fähnrich Wilhelm Beyerlein illustrates the intensity of operations during the last days of October. The *Gruppe* had transferred from Nagłowice, in Poland, on the 18th, and now its Fw 190s were deployed in bombing Soviet armour and positions immediately over the fronts facing Army Groups North and Centre.

In the eight days from 19–27 October, Beyerlein flew 11 missions including escort for four Ju 87s attacking tanks on the 19th. The next day, he scored a 'direct hit' on a tank despite heavy AA fire, with a second mission that afternoon against enemy vehicles, again in the teeth of fighter and AA fire. From 22 October, Beyerlein was airborne every day, including two sorties on the 24th and 26th, all against enemy positions, with attacks directed against Grosswattersdorf, Gnadenheim, Waldstück, Prassfeld, Pfälzerwalde, Petershausen, Amalienhof, Hopfenbruch and Oettingen. In that same period, Beyerlein lost three of his comrades killed and another posted missing.

ROCKETS

Despite the German view of the rocket as an anti-tank weapon being a generally negative one throughout World War 2, in the autumn of 1944, the Luftwaffe debuted a new ground-attack weapon for the *Schlachtflieger* intended primarily for use against armour. As Generalmajor Hitschhold explained in a post-war report;

'With the conversion of anti-tank [*Panzerjäger*] units to the Fw 190, three purely anti-tank *Gruppen* were to be formed with three *Staffeln* each. In addition, the third *Staffel* of every regular *Schlachtgruppe* was to become an anti-tank *Staffel*. The use of one or two anti-tank *Gruppen* together in an area of main effort was expected to produce good and lasting success.'

The first manifestation of a dedicated anti-tank rocket weapon emerged in early 1944 when trials commenced at the Luftwaffe's bomb- and explosive-testing ground at Udetfeld in Silesia. The trials used an adapted version of the Wehrmacht's 88 mm *Panzerschreck* ('Tank Fear') anti-tank weapon for airborne launching with electric discharge from Fw 190F-8/9s. The *Panzerschreck*, known officially as the *Raketenpanzerbüchse* (RPzB) 54, was a reusable, lightweight rocket-launcher intended for use by infantry and modelled on the American bazooka, examples of which had been captured from the US Army in Tunisia in 1943.

The head diameter of the *Panzerschreck* was 8.8 cm, it had a four-centimetre diameter rocket motor and a total combined weight of 7.1 kg. The hollow-charge warhead, known as the '*Puppehenkopf*' ('Doll's Head'), was contained in a sheet metal casing. The burning time of the rocket was 0.04 seconds, and it was to be fired from large, open-channel-section, sheet steel guide rails 1.5 m in length. The rockets were grouped in clusters of three and the rails were suspended from an ETC 50 or ETC 71 bomb rack for fitment beneath the wings of an Fw 190F-8.

In the early trials at Udetfeld, 12 *Panzerschreck* rockets were fitted to an Fw 190 and fired at targets from the close range of 45–180 m. The low velocity of 120–135 m per second meant that it was necessary to approach a target at very close range and at a decreased speed of 490 km/h, which greatly endangered both aircraft and pilot. For this reason, only a small number of rockets were ordered initially. It was found that a direct hit by one rocket was sufficient to set a tank alight, but to achieve this required three aircraft with full loads.

It is believed that the first unit to use the *Panzerschreck* was 1./SG 10, which began to take delivery of the weapon in the autumn of 1944. During November, this *Staffel* reported 23 Fw 190F-8s on strength and was based at Magyarmecske, 23 km southwest of Pécs in Hungary. Another early recipient of the rocket was 5./SG 77 under Oberleutnant Stephan Schmitt. The *Staffel* trained up at Udetfeld and then moved to Sarospatak in Hungary in early October. In one of its first operations with the *Panzerschreck*, the unit attacked Soviet tanks close to the Hungarian–Rumanian border, but Schmitt's Fw 190

The 88 mm RPzB 54, or *Panzerschreck*, anti-tank rocket weapon and shell, as used by ground forces. Fielded in an adapted form by some Luftwaffe *Schlachtstaffeln* in the East from late 1944, it proved disappointing in service (*Robert Forsyth Collection*)

was hit by enemy AA fire and the *Staffelkapitän* was killed. He was awarded the Knight's Cross posthumously on 29 October.

It is believed that 1.(Pz.) *Staffel* of dedicated anti-tank unit SG 9 was formed by redesignating 12.(Pz.)/SG 9 when it commenced conversion from the Hs 129 *Panzerjäger* to rocket-armed Fw 190s in November 1944. Other units understood to have taken delivery of the rocket in late 1944 included III./SG 3 at Frauenberg in Latvia, II./SG 2 and 8./SG 1, with further elements of SG 10 following in 1945.

The underwhelming performance of the early *Panzerschreck* prompted a revised weapon that still made use use of the ammunition of the first version due to stocks being readily available. Known as the *Panzerschreck II*, it featured a 275-mm-long hollow-charge warhead. The 157-mm long tail assembly carried the burner and four small, folding tail fins. The fins were each offset by two degrees, thus providing the spin necessary for stability. In tests, the warhead was found to penetrate up to 160 mm of tank armour.

In operational units, *Panzerschreck II* rockets, which were known officially as 'PD 8.8 cm *Pz. Büchsenrohr*', were suspended on individual underwing rails 328 mm apart in rows of six or eight rockets. Another method was also known to be used which saw two sets of two rockets mounted above each other suspended from an ETC 71 rack under the wing.

The advantage of the *Panzerschreck* lay in the fact that it was no longer necessary to attack a tank at its most vulnerable point – from the rear. However, the development and use of such an improvised weapon gave impetus to the development of the more sophisticated *Panzerblitz* rocket, which would see action for the first time not against the hordes of Soviet tanks advancing from the East, but rather, surprisingly, over the Western Front (see Chapter Seven).

On 1 December 1944, a study prepared by the RLM noted starkly that, 'The fast Fw 190 has so far been able to carry out its tasks on the Eastern Front without fighter escort, and because of its high performance can also, if necessary, perform the duties of an escort fighter for Ju 87 formations. With air supremacy in the hands of the enemy, the provision of fighter escorts is also necessary for Fw 190s because during the target approach, in climbing, and on account of their bombload, they are inferior in speed and manoeuvrability to the great number of enemy fighters employed. In addition to strong fighter escorts, the overwhelming enemy air superiority demands the concentration of all available ground-attack and fighter units for one task if success on the battlefield is to be won.

'The fighter escort is a decisive factor in the success of ground-attack operations. The strength of the escort is dependent on the situation and the type of aircraft employed, and it should be remembered that if Fw 190s have to act as fighter escort, the efficacy of these *Gruppen* as ground-attack units will be reduced.'

As 1945 loomed, so did the greatest challenges for the skills of the outnumbered *Schlachtflieger*, their Fw 190s and their impressive armament options on the Eastern Front.

Ground personnel, appearing somewhat perplexed, wait at the side of a crude taxiway somewhere in Italy in spring 1944, while behind them is an Fw 190F-8 of I./SG 4 (*EN Archive*)

CHAPTER SIX

THE SOUTH – LATE 1943–44

Bruised and battered, metaphorically, after the hard fighting in Sicily in the summer of 1943, German forces pulled back to the Italian mainland and, in doing so, readied themselves for the inevitable. In September and October, respectively, they evacuated the islands of Sardinia and Corsica. After the Italian Armistice was signed on 8 September, the Allied landings at Salerno commenced the following day, Naples fell on 1 October and on 1 December the German line along the River Sangro was breached. Slowly, doggedly, the Allies fought their way north towards Rome. By 12 January 1944, American troops had reached the River Garigliano, lying just ahead of the German Gustav Line.

The Luftwaffe, weakened by combat losses, deteriorating serviceability and disrupted supplies, marshalled its units under *Luftflotte* 2, commanded by Generalfeldmarschall von Richthofen. The air fleet's *Schlacht* element comprised just the Fw 190As, Fs and Gs of the *Stab*, I. and II./SG 4. The *Stab* had been formed at Piacenza, in northern Italy, at the time of reorganisation of the *Schlacht* force in October 1943 from *Stab*/Schl.G. 2, with command passing from Major Wolfgang Schenck to Major Heinrich Brücker. I./SG 4 at Guidonia under Major Werner Dörnbrack evolved from II./Schl.G. 2, while II./SG 4 was formed from II./SKG 10 also at Guidonia under the command of Hauptmann Gerhard Walther. At Guidonia, the Fw 190s were particularly well dispersed and camouflaged to the extent that the Germans believed the Allies were not aware they were there.

Serviceability at this time could be a problem depending on climatic conditions. Damp weather in northern Italy affected electrics on aircraft that were left continually in the open, while a shortage in spares arose because of transport difficulties. This meant that repairs could only be carried out at irregular intervals, and it was frequently necessary to make use of new aircraft to replace unserviceable ones which might have been repaired had spares been available.

Following the Allied landings in southern Italy in the autumn of 1943, SG 4 had mounted regular operations against enemy incursions, including strafing missions against supply columns that saw its Fw 190s flying as low as ten metres, or against warships in the Gulf of Naples when the Focke-Wulfs were loaded with a centreline 250-kg bomb as well as 50-kg weapons under each wing. On such anti-shipping missions, the Fw 190s would fly at sea level, pulling up to attack from about 20 m. In other instances, such as when attacking enemy airfields or transport columns, the offensive load comprised AB 500 containers loaded with one-kilogramme fragmentation bombs, which proved very effective.

In early January 1944, in a further illustration of how stretched Luftwaffe resources were, the *Stab* and I./SG 4 at Piacenza were slated for immediate transfer north, out of Italy, should an Allied invasion of Norway, Denmark or northwest Continental Europe take place. On 1 February, this contingency measure was refined, with both units shown as being based further north at Viterbo, but in the case of need, they were to move to Denain, in France.

According to *Luftflotte* 2's Chief of Staff, Oberst Törsten Christ, in the time immediately before the Allied landings at Anzio, to the south of Rome, in January, the principal mission of the force of around 30 Fw 190s of SG 4 was foreseen as providing close support to 10. and 14. *Armees* by conducting 'attacks against ground targets such as battle stations, vehicle concentrations and artillery positions, and by harassing the supply and reinforcement of Allied forces by attacks on ships being unloaded'.

However, the minimal fighter and reconnaissance forces available to *Fliegerführer* 2 (the tactical command based at Viterbo to the north of Rome) proved to be inadequate, and so the Luftwaffe was compelled to move forces south from its 'safer' northern airfields. That said, by early 1944, the adverse military situation in central Italy called for increased

The refuelling of Fw 190F-8 'White 1' of 1./SG 4 appears to be complete as members of the groundcrew move away the fuel hose and clamp shut the engine cowling at an airfield in Italy in 1944. The pilot sits in the cockpit and adjusts his earphones as he awaits instructions. The aircraft, which lacks ordnance, has a masked tail *Hakenkreuz* and partially overpainted fuselage theatre band and *Balkenkreuz* (*EN Archive*)

landing ground infrastructure to be prepared urgently for fighter units and *Schlachtgruppen* in the Rome and Viterbo areas, as well as further north in Perugia, Terni, Pisa, Florence and Siena.

As a result, following the landings at Anzio, which commenced with more than 36,000 Allied troops coming ashore on 22 January, the number of German fighters operating over the beachhead increased and the Luftwaffe was able to mount fighter patrols of 90–100 aircraft on occasion to counter the equivalent Allied patrols of 100–120 fighters. Simultaneously, this allowed I./SG 4 a reasonable opportunity to operate, but it took every effort on the part of the *Gruppe*'s groundcrews and pilots to mount one or two missions in a day.

During the afternoon of 24 January, SG 4 sent 15 Fw 190s to attack the Allied fleet off Anzio, followed by a second attack involving 43 aircraft that was carried out at dusk. The timing was opportune – some 33 Landing Ship, Tanks (LSTs) had just steamed up to Anzio, where they were subjected to the *Schlacht* attack. A 250-kg bomb struck the American destroyer USS *Plunkett* (DD-431), killing 13 crew and disabling its port engine. *Plunkett* survived the assault and escaped to Palermo. The light cruiser USS *Brooklyn* (CL-40) also escaped several near misses, as did the minesweeper USS *Prevail* (AM-107).

The next day *Luftflotte* 2 confirmed that it had conducted two operations on the 24th using 'ground-attack' aircraft against the enemy landing fleet off the beachhead. Operations had been hampered by weather, but in the first mission involving 19 'ground-attack aircraft' (the earlier-mentioned lower figure may have reflected 'aircraft on target') a direct hit had been scored on one vessel of 2500 tons which resulted in a 'violent explosion'. There had also been 'well-placed bomb hits on closely packed shipping in Anzio harbour and on unloadings. Effect not observed owing to low-lying cloud'.

On 26 January SG 4 launched another attack that damaged LST-366, seven patrol craft, two merchant vessels and a rescue tug. Christ described the *Schlachtflieger* operations against Allied shipping as being undertaken 'in the face of formidable defensive fire'.

When attacking shipping with bombs off the coast of Italy, the customary tactic adopted by the Fw 190s of approaching their targets in a shallow, line-astern glide was abandoned in favour of steep, high-speed dives similar to that used by the Ju 87 units. After release, the *Schlachtflieger* would level out and fly low across the target area, using cannon where appropriate. This method was also eventually abandoned and replaced by single-aircraft, free-form, tip-and-run-style attacks.

On 23 March, an appraisal by the RAF's No 276 (Signals) Wing noted, 'A new development in the fighter-bomber situation has been the apparent operational use of two *Gruppen*. W/T [Wireless Telegraphy] intercepts show that 31 Fw 190s were sent from Piacenza to Rieti between March 10th and 21st, and a further 11 were sent during the same period to Viterbo. Take-off and landing messages on W/T also indicate that formations are composed of two groups of aircraft, which might reasonably be supposed to be taking off from two separate aerodromes. In any case, the large number of Fw 190s employed in single missions – 28 operated in a single day against Cassino on the 19th – could hardly be supplied by one *Gruppe*.'

That month (March), I. and II./SG 4 were assigned to the contingent Luftwaffe defence force ready to move to Bulgaria under '*Gertrud*' (see Chapter Five) in the eventuality that the Allies used neutral Turkish territory to attack Bulgaria. The *Stab* and I./SG 4 would move to Melekli and II./SG 4 to Malevo, but this threat never materialised.

During April and May, the *Schlachtgruppen* suffered steadily mounting losses at the hands of Allied fighters, even though each *Gruppe* was often provided with fighter escort of double its own number. For the most part, losses occurred after diving attacks when, because of the variance in performance between the Fw 190s and their Bf 109 escorts (the Fw 190 being slower in the climb) and also as a result of aerial combat, the Focke-Wulfs frequently became separated from their escort and thus vulnerable. Furthermore, Fw 190s on their way to, or returning from, the Cassino Front were exposed to flank attacks by Allied fighters approaching from the coast around Anzio. The Focke-Wulfs also had to maintain a straight course for fear of running out of fuel over lengthy distances, which did not help matters.

On 7 April, Hauptmann Heinrich Zwipf, the recently appointed replacement for Dörnbrack as *Kommandeur* of I./SG 4, was killed on the *Gruppe*'s airfield at Rieti when it came under attack by RAF Kittyhawks of No 112 Sqn just as a flight of Fw 190s was in the process of taking off. Zwipf was piloting one of two Focke-Wulfs that were shot down – his aircraft was airborne but crashed moments later. An Eastern Front Stuka veteran with hundreds of missions under his belt, Zwipf had previously served as *Staffelkapitän* of 3./StG 77. He had commenced conversion training to the Fw 190 shortly after the October 1943 reorganisation, and was awarded the Knight's Cross on 31 December that same year. The other pilot shot down was Unteroffizier Kurt Fischer of 1./SG 4, who was also killed.

The unit carried out strafing missions in the Cassino and Gaeta areas on 3 May. Fifteen days later, the commander of II./SG 4, Hauptmann Walther, was killed following combat with two Spitfires east of Viterbo. After claiming one of them shot down, Walther was forced to bail out of his own aircraft near Scandriglia. In doing so, he apparently knocked himself unconscious against the tailplane and failed to open his parachute.

With a 500-kg bomb suspended from its ETC 501 rack, Fw 190 'Black 9' awaits clearance to taxi out for another mission over Italy. The groundcrewman grips the leading edge of the starboard wing, ready to offer further guidance to the pilot. The aircraft features I./SG 4's Mickey Mouse emblem on its nose (*EN Archive*)

Walther was an accomplished airman, former *Zerstörer* pilot and *Gruppe* Adjutant of II./SKG 10. He had also been seconded to a high-altitude fighter and *Zerstörer* test unit. Mentioned in the Wehrmacht daily communique on 24 March for his actions over the Cassino Front, Walther had been awarded the Knight's Cross two days later after completing 300 missions.

21 May was a particularly black day for SG 4, when it lost seven Fw 190s from 3., 5. and 6. *Staffeln* to Spitfires over the Rome and Viterbo areas. The casualties included Oberleutnant Robert Reiprich, *Staffelkapitän* of 3./SG 4, who crashed east of the Italian capital, and Hauptmann Rolf Strössner, a *Legion Condor* veteran and fighter pilot who had flown with JGs 27 and 1 earlier in the war. But worse was to come when the recently appointed *Geschwaderkommodore*, Major Georg Dörffel, was killed in action on 26 May while attacking Allied bombers northwest of Rome. Like Gerhard Walther, he bailed out of his Fw 190 but struck its tailplane. Dörffel had flown 1004 combat missions in the Hs 123, Bf 109 and Fw 190, and had been awarded the Oak Leaves to the Knight's Cross on 14 April 1943. He was posthumously promoted to Oberstleutnant.

The reality was that operations by the *Schlachtstaffeln* in declining numbers resulting from punishing losses were unviable and purposeless, as *General der Flieger* Maximilian Ritter von Pohl, at the time the *General der Deutschen Luftwaffe in Mittelitalien*, explained;

'On 11 May, the enemy commenced its spring offensive, and on 17 May this led to their breakthrough at Cassino. During this period, despite a superb degree of operational willingness on the part of the aircrews, it was no longer possible to deploy the *Schlachtflieger* force (30 *Schlacht* aircraft and 50 fighters to provide escort), without them becoming diverted into air combat with superior enemy forces.

'After a few such operations, which were useless for the Army, and led to serious losses for the air units, no further *Schlachtflieger* operations were undertaken with bombs, and the Fw 190 *Gruppen* were converted to the fighter role to provide protection for rear areas. But even these operations had to be abandoned when, towards the end of May, the two *Gruppen* were pulled back to Piacenza for re-equipping in order to be transferred quickly to the coasts of southern France or the English Channel in case of an Allied invasion.'

On 27 May, in what must have been one of SG 4's final missions in Italy, 2. *Fliegerdivision* reported that four Fw 190s had conducted anti-shipping patrols and another three had undertaken reconnaissance sorties. By the end of the day, one Focke-Wulf had been posted missing and another had been shot down and its pilot killed. The latter was probably the Fw 190G-8 flown by Leutnant Otto Kallenberger of 6./SG 4, who clashed with Spitfires over Amelia.

On 31 May, I./SG 4 reported 14 Fw 190s on strength, of which four were serviceable, while II./SG 4 listed 27, with nine serviceable. In addition, the *Geschwaderstab* had three aircraft, of which two were ready. In June, the remaining elements of SG 4 were moved east from Piacenza to Airasca and Levaldigi, and while new Fw 190s did arrive at these airfields, it was to no purpose. At the end of June, the *Geschwader* began its relocation to southeast Latvia.

Meanwhile, SG 4's III. *Gruppe* had been based in France since November, but it was hardly surprising that given I. and II. *Gruppen*'s experiences in Italy, by late spring 1944, Generalmajor Hitschhold was concerned about III./SG 4's prospects against any Allied invasion that might come in France.

CHAPTER SEVEN

THE WEST – 1944

Groundcrew steer an LWC 500 hydraulic bomb trolley beneath an Fw 190G-2 from I./SKG 10, the aircraft also having been fitted with 300-litre drop tanks for long-range missions. The weapon appears to be a 500-kg SD 500 *Splitterbombe* intended for use against buildings and 'ironwork', such as ships. Although a fragmentation weapon, the SD 500 was considered a *Mehrzweckbombe* (multi-purpose bomb). Like the Fw 190s of I./SKG 10, the Focke-Wulfs of III./SG 4 operated in very similar conditions against the Allied invasion fleet off Normandy for a brief period in June 1944 (*EN Archive*)

As mentioned in the previous two chapters, the Luftwaffe's need to deploy most of its *Schlachtgeschwadern* on the Eastern Front resulted initially in just one *Gruppe* being sent to the West – even less than was based to Italy. Indeed, it was a *Gruppe* of SG 4, the bulk of which was in Italy, which was transferred to France in November 1943.

III./SG 4 had been formed at Graz on 1 November 1943 from III./SKG 10 following the reorganisation of the ground-attack units in October 1943 and after the latter *Gruppe* had relocated from Italy. The *Stab*, 9., 10. and 11./SKG 10 became, respectively, *Stab*, 7., 8. and 9./SG 4. Placed under the command of Major Werner Dedekind, the *Gruppe* had no aircraft assigned to it upon establishment, and unlike the *Geschwaderstab*, I. and II. *Gruppen*, it was not moved south, but instead to Beaumont-sur-Oise, to the north of Paris. It arrived here on 20 November, whereupon the *Gruppe* commenced very basic training.

Still awaiting aircraft, III./SG 4 remained there until 30 November, when it relocated 160 km northeast to Laon-Athies. Here, it was more of the same, although two members of the *Gruppe* were summoned to the *General der Schlachtflieger* just before Christmas to discuss the unit's future assignment and its equipping.

On 16 January 1944, an advance detachment under Leutnant Herbert Eissele of 3./SG 4 set out for Clastres airfield, 15 km south of Saint-Quentin, to inspect facilities there with a view to a further move.

Simultaneously, seven pilots were sent to Königsberg to collect Fw 190s for the *Gruppe*, which had been placed under the tactical jurisdiction of II. *Fliegerkorps*. On the 30th, Major Gerhard Weyert formally took over command of the unit from Major Dedekind. Weyert had flown the Ju 87 with the *Legion Condor* in Spain before transferring to the *Legion*'s fighter *Staffel*. A recipient of the Spanish Cross in Gold, he later flew Bf 110s with II./ZG 1 and II./ZG 2.

On 31 January 1944, Weyert met with General Alfred Bülowius, commander of II. *Fliegerkorps*, who informed the new *Kommandeur* of the not welcome news that all the assigned Fw 190s intended for III./SG 4 presently at Le Bourget were to be transferred to Viterbo for deployment with I. and II./SG 4. This was in addition to a number of III. *Gruppe* personnel who were sent to Italy to gain operational experience, as well as others who had been 'poached' for bomber units such as I./KG 66 – a *Gruppe* taking part in the new bombing campaign directed at the British Isles from bases in France.

On 1 February, III./SG 4 was slated for immediate transfer to Mons-en-Chausse 'with all operational elements, including those in preparation', should any Allied landings in northwest Continental Europe take place. By the 10th, the *Gruppe* had moved into Clastres, having transferred by road. It quickly commenced building blast shelters, although 8. *Staffel* was billeted eight kilometres away in the village of Frière.

As much training as possible that could be conducted *without* aircraft continued, and by 20 February, despite the unit still lacking Focke-Wulfs, it reported 30 pilots on strength, of whom seven were ferrying Fw 190s to the *Geschwader*'s *Gruppen* based in Italy. Finally, however, by the end of March, III./SG 4 reported 31 Fw 190A-6s and three A-7/R6s as having been delivered, and this was sufficient to set up an organised routine of more in-depth operational training that included dummy strafing runs and dive attacks conducted over western France.

Back in Germany, the *Schlachtflieger* were coming under pressure in the battle for resources. Generalleutnant Adolf Galland, commander of the Jagdwaffe, was having to scrape the barrel for manpower for daylight defence of the Reich. While at a two-day conference with Göring over 15–16 May, he proposed that II./SG 2, which was then fighting in the Crimea, be converted over to fighter operations.

His rationale was that the *Gruppe* numbered 11 pilots, each credited with between five and 90 aerial victories. Their capabilities would be valued by the *Jagdgruppen* fighting the Allied air forces over northwest Europe. Göring refused, but Galland continued to press. If that was not possible, then he suggested the *Schlachtflieger* should release all pilots with more than five victories. Again, Göring demurred, decreeing that ground-attack pilots could only transfer voluntarily.

Meanwhile, training continued within III./SG 4 in an uninterrupted and routine way for the next few weeks, including instruction on flying with drop tanks. On 20 May, the Fw 190s of 9./SG 4 were detached to Le Luc, in the south of France, for some generally fruitless anti-submarine patrols over the Mediterranean. This '*U-Bootbekämpfung*' continued until 3 June, when 9. *Staffel* returned to Clastres, after which things changed dramatically, although not unexpectedly.

On the 6th, the Allies landed in France, pouring 155,000 men, plus vehicles, onto the Normandy beaches in Operation *Overlord*. The Allied air cover was immense, with sufficient capability to fly more than 14,500 sorties within the first 24 hours.

On the eve of the invasion, III./SG 4 reported 38 Fw 190s on strength, of which 25 were operationally ready. As the Luftwaffe reactively scrambled to rush its fighters into France from the Reich, the Fw 190s of III./SG 4 were amongst the relatively small number of single-engined 'fighters' on hand to strike at the freshly landed Allied forces. Contrary to the popular belief that the Luftwaffe effectively 'failed to appear' in the first days of *Overlord*, while its presence was, admittedly, low-key, those crews who did sortie did the best they could.

Firstly, however, on 6 June, III./SG 4 transferred from Clastres to Laval, its designated forward airfield in Normandy, west of Le Mans. From there, it was possible for bomb-carrying Fw 190s to reach the five landing beaches. But even as the first seven Fw 190s made their transfer flight carrying mechanics in their aircraft fuselages shortly after midday, they encountered between 12–15 USAAF P-51s over Bretigny, 30 km south of Paris.

In the combat that followed, Oberleutnant Johann Pühringer, the *Gruppe* Adjutant, was shot down in flames and killed in his Fw 190A-7, while Leutnant Gerhard Limberg and Unteroffizier Max Rahofer, flying an A-7 and an A-6, respectively, were also shot down but escaped either unhurt or with light wounds. The condition of their luckless mechanics was not known.

Just before 1600 hrs, eight more Fw 190s took off for Laval, but they also encountered 15 enemy fighters near Saint-Jean d'Asse, north of Le Mans. Hauptmann Heinz Mihlan was shot down and managed to exit his Fw 190A-6 unharmed but Feldwebel Franz Brauneis was killed. Unteroffizier Wenzel force-landed unharmed near Rouen but Feldwebel Eidam and Unteroffizier Paul Ebert were also later reported as lost. It was an ominous and inauspicious beginning to the *Gruppe*'s operations.

Then, at 1719 hrs, four Fw 190s, led by Oberleutnant Heinrich Hesse, *Staffelkapitän* of 9./SG 4, took off on what was probably the *Gruppe*'s debut mission over the beaches.

Armourers, believed to be from SG 4, prepare to haul an LWC 500 hydraulic bomb trolley laden with a 500-kg SC 500 *Minenbombe* towards an Fw 190 in its blast pen. *Minenbomben* were used against fixed targets such as airfield installations and bridges, as well as large maritime targets. The man at centre is holding a *Schloss* 500/XII connector/adaptor which secured the bomb to the Fw 190's centreline ETC 501 rack. Note the Oberfeldwebel at left wearing binoculars, probably to keep a watch on the sky above for Allied fighters (*EN Archive*)

Since mid-May, the tactical doctrine for bomb-carrying Fw 190s against enemy invasion forces in France had been established based on experience gained by I. and II./SG 4 in Sicily and off the Italian coast in 1943 and early 1944. OKL envisaged missions being carried out in *Gruppe* strength and, when possible, under fighter escort. The approach flight was to be made 'in a relatively closed-up formation, each *Staffel* echeloned back to the right of a single line, with three *Staffeln* forming a *Gruppe* "Vic" closed up'.

Furthermore, the approach flight was not to be made 'under 4000 m because fighter opposition is to be expected. Attacks by Fw 190 units, after closing up in a *Gruppe* formation, will be accomplished from as steep a dive as possible from the attack formation, after going into a dive straight ahead or after peeling off to the left from a *Staffel* echeloned to the right and well closed up to the front. In details, the conduct of the attack depends on the type and situation of the target. With the Fw 190, diving is possible up to 80 degrees with 885 km/h terminal velocity.'

This was a fine theory, but the reality facing Oberleutnant Hesse, with just three comrades, at 1745 hrs on 6 June as he swept over *Juno* Beach at Saint-Aubin-sur-Mer, where the 8th Canadian Infantry Brigade and No 48 (Royal Marine) Commando were landing, was very different. To get to the enemy fleet meant flying through strong light and medium AA fire, and also evading some 12 patrolling Typhoons and Spitfires. Nevertheless, the four Fw 190s commenced their dives from 1500 m.

When targeting shipping, Luftwaffe pilots devised a form of attack known as *Steckrübenwerf* ('the turnip attack'). When approaching a target from the beam, the method was to approach a ship at very low level, almost at surface-level, and at about a range of 900 m pull up to 45–90 m, according to the height of the vessel, using full throttle. Just ahead of that, the pilot would make a short strafing run and release his bomb just before pulling up and flying as low over the target as possible. The same principle could be used in making attacks from ahead or astern, but in doing so the threat of ship-mounted AA guns was minimised. The ship was approached at an angle of around ten degrees from its long axis and the bomb dropped near the side of the vessel. The exit flight was made at low level along the long axis of the ship.

The four Fw 190s led by Hesse were carrying SC 500 bombs, and they dived down to 600 m. Two landing craft were claimed as hit and destroyed. All aircraft returned to base. That evening, Leutnant Karl-Ludwig Klepke of 9. *Staffel* led a similar attack with four aircraft using the same tactics. The Fw 190s dropped bombs on vehicles on the bridge at Bénouville, near Ouistreham, amidst light AA fire, and also managed to avoid formations of Spitfires, Mustangs and Thunderbolts present during the attack. One Focke-Wulf was hit by ground fire and badly damaged. After departing the target area, the Fw 190s were forced to land at Rennes as a result of the presence of enemy fighters.

Finally, in the gathering dusk, Oberleutnant Hesse took off once more from Laval at 2100 hrs, leading five Fw 190s to strike at enemy landing points at Lion-sur-Mer, a short way west along *Sword* Beach from Ouistreham. Thirty minutes later, because of intense AA fire and the presence of 50 Allied fighters, the German pilots had to drop their SC 500s on an alternative target. One Fw 190 was badly damaged by ground fire and the results of the bombing could not be ascertained because of the strong enemy fighter defence, but there were no losses among the SG 4 pilots, and they returned to the alternative field at Angers.

During the course of the next day (7 June), as the Allies fought to consolidate their beachheads, III./SG 4 attempted four missions against various targets on the landing beaches and in the immediate beachhead area. This time conditions were much harder, with the Allies mounting a massive and almost impenetrable fighter screen. Leutnant Günter Esau of

7./SG 4 led the first group of five Fw 190s up at dawn, but they encountered seven P-51s north of Caen and were unable to reach the target. As a result of the combat with the P-51s, Esau and Oberleutnant Friedrich Kellner of 7. *Staffel* were both wounded but able to return to Laval.

At 0845 hrs, the *Kommandeur*, Major Weyert, was at the head of ten Fw 190s which managed to reach enemy targets at Riva Bella on *Sword* Beach 40 minutes later, where they dived from 2000 m down to 500 m, dropping seven SC 500s and three SC 250s. One landing craft was destroyed and two bombs exploded amongst vehicles on shore. One Focke-Wulf was hit by AA fire, but the pilot was unharmed and all aircraft returned.

Leutnant Klepke led the third mission of the day, taking off from Laval with four other Fw 190s at 1535 hrs, heading for the British landing beaches. It was to prove an abortive effort, for they ran into a formation of Mustangs on their approach and had to carry out an emergency release of their bombs. No losses were suffered, but having been pursued by P-51s, the Fw 190s had to land at Tours. It was, frustratingly, more of the same for the final mission of the day when Oberleutnant Hesse took off at 1830 hrs with a *Schwarm* of Fw 190s to bomb the beaches. Once again the Germans were blocked by approximately 28 Mustangs and were forced to drop their bombs off target (inland southeast of Bayeux), but there were no losses.

III./SG 4 continued its pace of operations on 8 June, mounting three missions involving 17 sorties. At 1240 hrs eight Fw 190s took off from Laval with Major Weyert leading, but they had only got as far as Argentan when they were intercepted by Spitfires and Mustangs and forced to jettison their bombs early. Feldwebel Krüger managed to hit and badly damage a P-51 and the *Gruppe* avoided any casualties. Later that afternoon, Oberleutnant Hesse led four Fw 190s to attack the bridges over the Caen Canal. They were over the target at 1700 hrs, and despite light and medium AA fire, they dived from 1200 m to 300 m and were able to drop two SD 500 fragmentation bombs and an SC 250, which apparently hit the target. Two large explosions were seen. Also, despite ever-present USAAF fighters, they all returned home without loss.

Then, at 1950 hrs Weyert was back up in the air leading five Fw 190s to attack Allied shipping off Riva Bella in the now crowded beachhead. On this occasion, the *Schlachtflieger* were joined by three fighter pilots from Fw 190-equipped I./JG 11 based at Rennes and led by Leutnant Hans Schrangel, *Staffelkapitän* of 3./JG 11.

Weyert had told II. *Fliegerkorps* back in February that fighter escort was beneficial for *Schlacht* aircraft since it meant that an attack could be carried out 'closed up' rather than in a dispersed formation, meaning that a greater chance of inflicting damage was possible. Equally, JG 11, like other fighter units now transferred to France from the Reich, was already conducting *Jabo* missions over the beachhead area.

Northwest of Riva Bella, the small, combined formation of Fw 190s sighted three large freighters of around 3000 tonnes each and 20 landing craft. At 2035 hrs the Focke-Wulfs dived down from 1800 m, descending to 700 m, each dropping an SC 500. Weyert later reported, 'Bombs were well on target, but closer effect not possible to observe due to strong Flak and fighter defence'.

Having dropped their bombs, the Focke-Wulf pilots managed to conduct some hasty reconnaissance and must have been struck by the sheer strength of the Allied force landing in Normandy. North of Riva Bella and Lion-sur-Mer, they observed '2 extraordinarily large landing formations, with between 3–5 freighters of 3–5,000 BRT, 20 landing craft of 300 BRT and 80 small landing craft, a small cruiser and around 4 km to the north, 1 aircraft carrier'. This in addition to fighter patrols in the immediate vicinity of around '80 Spitfires, Mustangs, Lightnings and Thunderbolts'.

The Luftwaffe formation returned without loss, but the stark reality of what lay ahead must have been daunting to the German airmen.

III./SG 4 soldiered on in Normandy for another ten days or so, but over 18–19 June it was ordered south to Clermont-Ferrand, some 600 km from Laval and the Invasion Front. There, for a brief period, the *Gruppe* re-equipped with Fw 190F-8s and carried out attacks on suspected or known locations of *Maquis* groups in central France. During July, unit strength was reported as being four remaining Fw 190A-6s and 49 F-8s. On 3 July, the *Gruppe* commenced preparations for a move to Latvia, where it would join the rest of SG 4 to fly missions in support of Army Groups North and Centre. In the course of the next few months, in what was a 'fighting retreat', the Fw 190s played a crucial role in the Luftwaffe's efforts to stem the Soviet advance through East Prussia.

Meanwhile, there had been a change in command of SG 4 on 23 June when Oberstleutnant Ewald Janssen was formally appointed *Kommodore*. Janssen had had an eclectic service career, having seen service with the *Legion Condor* during the Spanish Civil War, after which he flew Ju 87s with StGs 1 and 2 and had also instructed on the Stuka, before taking command of Bf 109-equipped I./JG 300 and then JG 302 in the defence of the Reich.

MORE ROCKETS

From November 1944 trials commenced with a new anti-tank rocket for the *Schlachtgeschwadern* following disappointment with the *Panzerschreck*. The first incarnation of a series of three variants developed by the Deutsche Waffen und Munitionsfabrik, the *Panzerblitz* ('Tank Lightning') *I* carried a hollow-charge warhead identical to the *Panzerschreck* but fitted with a ballistic cap. The warhead had a relatively small explosive content of around 590 g and the 208 mm-long body featured four slightly offset sheet metal fins. The rocket weighed seven kilogrammes, its trajectory was long and flat and its dispersion pattern was good. The all-burnt velocity was 320–340 m per second, with a burning time of between 0.4 and 0.8 seconds. This enabled an Fw 190 laden with 12 rockets to fire at a range of 200–300 m.

The *Einzelschussgerät Panzerblitz* (EG-Pb) one-time discharge device was made by Curt Heber of Osterode. It comprised a guide rail into which the lugs of the *Panzerblitz* slid from the front end when loading. The EG-Pb could be connected rigidly to an ETC 50 underwing rack using an intermediate carrier, and offered little air resistance. In case of an emergency, the pilot could jettison the *Panzerblitz*, the EG-Pb and the intermediate carrier from the ETC 50 by operating the standard bomb release gear.

In trials, as many single rails as was practically and aerodynamically possible were placed side-by-side beneath an aircraft's wing. Initially,

A wooden mock fitment of four PD 8.8 cm *Panzerschreck II* launch tubes suspended from ETC 71 underwing racks beneath the wing of an Fw 190F-8 (*EN Archive*)

projectiles were discharged as single rounds, but during the course of testing it proved effective to join several EG-Pbs into a rail system. From this, the *Abschussschienegerät*-Pb (AG-Pb) was devised, which consisted of a system of six or eight rails fixed beneath an aircraft's wing by four screws.

In initial flights, six *Panzerblitz I* rockets were carried beneath each wing of an Fw 190, and they could be fired in salvos of three, six or 12. The loss in speed with racks fitted was around 15 km/h, and when loaded with missiles this increased to around 30 km/h.

In order to determine the lead angle, the pilot of an Fw 190 would have to reduce his speed to around 490 km/h (by lowering his aircraft's undercarriage if necessary) shortly before firing. Compared to the *Panzerschreck*, the *Panzerblitz* could be launched at twice the range – about 200 m. The projectiles could not be discharged all at once due to their close proximity, as the exhaust could cause interference. They were instead discharged in single rounds or in a series, with at least 70 m interval between the individual projectiles, by means of an automatic firing device. A projectile reached its maximum speed after only 0.8 seconds. In tests conducted at Tarnewitz, a strike rate of one hit in six was attained on a 10 × 10 m target at 250 m.

At the beginning of November 1944, after numerous revised orders, the pilots of III./SG 4 were told to move west from Tukums, in Latvia, to Udetfeld, while the *Gruppe*'s groundcrews were to go to Eichwalde. An exception was a small, advance detachment of armourers and aircraft technicians who would travel to Udetfeld to be briefed on the *Panzerblitz*. SG 4 would be the first *Schlachtgruppe* to receive the rocket.

On 2 November, the *Kommandeur*, Major Weyert, flew to Berlin-Rangsdorf, where he met with the *General der Schlachtflieger*, Generalmajor Hitschhold, and Oberstleutnant Druschel from his Staff to discuss the use of the *Panzerblitz* with his *Gruppe*. Hitschhold had expressed his concerns to Göring about the injudiciousness of operating *Schlachtgruppen* in the West without fighter cover. The Reichsmarschall offered a vague promise about making fighters available for the task, and the day after his meeting with Hitschhold, Weyert met with Oberst Lothar von Heinemann, Chief of Staff of II. *Jagdkorps*, the tactical fighter command on the Western Front, to go over 'operational principles' for the new weapon.

Over the next few days, 27 selected pilots from III./SG 4 commenced trial firings

A six-channel AG-Pb underwing launch rack for *Panzerblitz I* rockets has been fitted to this Fw 190F of an unidentified unit. The rack was referred to by some Luftwaffe personnel as the '*Gartenzaun*' ('Garden Fence') (*EN Archive*)

over the range at Udetfeld against captured tanks. Weyert arrived there on 7 November, and together with Oberleutnant Hans Busch, *Staffelkapitän* of 7./SG 4, met with Major Herbert Eggers of E.Kdo 26, an anti-tank weapons testing unit formed in January 1944 from 11.(Pz.)/SG 9 that had carried out trials with the *Panzerschreck*. It was agreed that nine of the *Gruppe*'s armourers should be sent to Curt Heber for a one-day course, after which Eggers envisaged they should be adequately familiarised with the *Panzerblitz*.

Training was dogged by bad weather, and so time was spent in the 'classroom' on tank recognition and studying technical manuals. Although Eggers 'donated' four of E.Kdo 26's Fw 190s to III./SG 4, this, in reality, was of little practical help because of the lack of *Panzerblitz* rockets. Weyert spoke with a representative of Curt Heber who was also at Udetfeld and pressed him to assist in accelerating production of the first series of rockets, as well as looking at ways in which to simplify aspects of the firing system. However, the expected first four launching sets had still not arrived by 11 November, so Weyert persuaded the Curt Heber representative to go to Osterode to investigate.

Meanwhile, ten new Fw 190F-8s had been made available for III./SG 4 at Reinsehlen, near Soltau, which made a total of 49 Focke-Wulfs. But as the *Gruppe* war diarist remarked, 'Since the plan is to go to the West, it is necessary to significantly improve *Panzerblitz* firing skills and to ensure intensive formation training'.

On 17 November, Weyert again met with Hitschhold, Druschel and Eggers. The War Diary noted;

'The *Kommandeur* explained that training has suffered from the persistently bad weather and ever-increasing damage to the [rocket] launch racks. The hit results are completely unacceptable – 5% overall, 3% hits on the firing range. At least two full flying days of five hours per pilot are needed for the training of all pilots in firing the *Panzerblitz*, as well as formation and fighter flying at Reinsehlen.'

For his part, in 1945, Generalmajor Hitschhold favoured the *Panzerblitz I* over the *Panzerschreck*, and recalled to British interrogators, 'It was possible to fire the rockets either in salvos of three, six or all 12 at once. The attacks were delivered at very close range, from 50 to 200 m, and depending on the defence, my pilots chose whether to fire all their rounds in one run or not. If the defence was weak, they made several attacks, and they always preferred to attack with several aircraft. It required three aircraft, firing their full loads, to ensure the knocking out of one tank – so one hit in 36. Pilots had little training, however, but I think they improved things to something approaching one hit in 24. We were working on equipping the aircraft with more rockets so that each aircraft could reckon on one kill per sortie.

'I never experienced any danger from my own rockets unless a tank blew up from a direct hit. The pilots were at least trained to turn away immediately after firing. Usually, every direct hit resulted in setting a tank on

A rare photograph showing six *Panzerblitz* missiles loaded into the improved short-length projector rails of an underwing launch rack on a crash-landed Fw 190. Those *Staffeln* deploying the rocket operationally would use the abbreviation 'Pb' on reports, logbooks and orders of battle to denote rocket use (*EN Archive*)

Hubertus Hitschhold, seen here as a Major at the time of the award of the Oak Leaves to the Knight's Cross, was Oberst Dr. Ernst Kupfer's successor as *General der Schlachtflieger*. Above his left-side tunic pocket is the *Schlachtflieger* flight clasp, which was instituted in April 1944. Hitschhold was a proponent of the use of rocket weapons for the *Schlacht* units, particularly the *Panzerblitz*. He told the Allies, 'We achieved good results with rockets against locomotives and soft vehicles, but I preferred using cannon against the latter' (*EN Archive*)

fire either immediately or very shortly afterwards, depending on where the hit had occurred. The crew of the tank was generally killed immediately, and that was attributed to either blast or splinters within the tank.

'We did not try making steep dive-attacks because of the short range which was required by the high dispersion of the rocket, and in a steep dive the tendency was to fire at too long a range, with a resulting inability to gain a hit. We attacked up- and downwind as far as possible in a 20-degree dive. If tanks were parked up, we generally elected to use bombs.

'We used the *Revi* sight with a "ladder" graticule, and used our guns on the run-up because Russian infantry usually rode on the outside of their tanks and put up sporadic small arms resistance. We also achieved good results with rockets against locomotives and soft vehicles, but I preferred using cannon against the latter.'

For the rest of November, III./SG 4 endured bad weather, disruption from changing base airfields, inadequate facilities, technical problems and Allied air attacks. It is believed that *Panzerblitz* rockets were used for the first time on 7 December when the *Gruppe* attacked enemy vehicles in the Strasbourg–Hagenau area. One Fw 190 failed to return and all the others were damaged by AA fire. Weyert viewed the mission as a failure, and proposed attacking only less-defended targets in future.

One positive was that I./SG 4 arrived at Köln-Ostheim from Latvia on 20 December, staging via Stubendorf and Ziegenhain. It had 33 Fw 190F-8s. II./SG 4 arrived simultaneously at Bonn-Hangelar.

For much of December 1944, the weather over the Western Front had precluded any significant operations by either the Luftwaffe or Allied air forces. Aircraft lay grounded on airfields shrouded in fog.

In his entry for 15 December, the III./SG 4 war diarist noted, 'The great German offensive in the West has begun. Winter battles in the West'. In fact, what was to be the last German offensive in the West began at 0530 hrs on 16 December. It was a plan so audacious that no senior Allied commander expected it. Codenamed Operation *Wacht am Rhein* ('Watch on the Rhine'), it had been devised by Hitler, who wanted to drive an armoured wedge between the Allies by thrusting through the forests and hill country of the Belgian Ardennes to retake Antwerp. He also hoped that he could trap the US First and Ninth Armies around Aachen, thus eliminating the threat posed to the Ruhr.

There were further frustrating delays to SG 4's operations, but at last, on 22 December, a *Geschwader*-strength bombing operation was planned against the key Belgian town of Bastogne. At 0730 hrs the next morning, all three *Gruppen* were placed at half-hour readiness. Fighter escort was to be provided by JG 2. At 1020 hrs, the first 14 Fw 190s took off, but just 16 minutes later they were recalled by the *Kommodore*, Oberstleutnant Janssen. At 1038, however, this order was revoked. Two minutes later, the pilots received a counter-order – the aircraft were to return.

In a dangerous but farcical situation, radio contact between the Fw 190s failed, and due to the non-appearance of the fighter escort, the *Kommandeur* had turned back independently, landing at 1110 hrs. Ten minutes later, strong enemy fighter and bomber formations passed over the airfield. New orders were issued for take-off at 1340 hrs, but between 1325–1345 hrs, around 30 Allied fighter-bombers attacked the airfield and its buildings. Astonishingly, there was no loss of aircraft or personnel, but SG 4's attempt to execute an operation on the 22nd had failed.

Next day, Christmas Eve, at 0745 hrs, II. and III./SG 4 were again placed on the 22nd readiness for a further effort to return to Bastogne to bomb the American forces trapped there by the advance of SS-*Oberstgruppenführer* Josef 'Sepp' Dietrich's 6. *Panzer Armee*. Seven Fw 190s of III./SG 4 took off at 0855 hrs, with aircraft from II. *Gruppe* following 15 minutes later. It then took 25 minutes to rendezvous and assemble with the assigned fighter escort. The mission was accomplished, but on the return flight, the fighters became engaged with P-47s and P-51s, and very quickly the Luftwaffe machines were compelled to break off due to fuel limitations. This resulted in the *Schlachtflieger* being forced to disperse – three Focke-Wulfs landed at Köln-Wahn, one force-landed at Sinzig, south of Bonn, and two at Bonn-Hangelar. Oberfähnrich Zotlötterer failed to return and the aircraft of Oberleutnant Eissele was badly shot up.

A further mission was scheduled for the afternoon, but the planned fighter escort became involved in intercepting USAAF heavy bombers returning to England and so the operation was cancelled.

An inventory of III./SG 4's scattered aircraft on 25 December found 20 Fw 190s at Wahn (of which 11 were operationally ready), six at Göttingen, four at Kirtorf, 11 at Reinsehlen, one at Krefeld and one at Kassel-Rothwesten. Three aircraft had failed to return from operations, six were damaged in some way and three were suffering from severe battle damage.

During the early morning of the 26th, seven Fw 190s of III./SG 4 carried out an attack on American positions in forests around Bastogne, and at 0755 hrs on the 27th, ten of the *Gruppe*'s Focke-Wulfs took off alongside aircraft of I. and II. *Gruppen* in a return to Bastogne to bomb troop assemblies, the formation being led by the *Kommandeur* of I./SG 4, Major Dörnbrack. However, at some point in the mission, Dörnbrack's aircraft suffered engine failure and he was forced to turn back, but as he did so, he was followed by the rest of the formation. Unable to hear Dörnbrack's instructions, the pilots of I. and II./SG 4 dropped their bombs over German territory, while some of III. *Gruppe* returned with bombs still attached to their aircraft.

Following a rapid refuelling and rearming, a second mission to Bastogne was attempted after midday, but the Fw 190s were recalled 20 minutes later to avoid a large approaching incursion of USAAF bombers and escort fighters – two P-51s duly strafed the airfield.

For the next few days, the worsening weather prevented any flying. On the 29th, Oberstleutnant Janssen, who had been awarded the Knight's Cross on 31 October 1944 in recognition for completing around 400 missions and claiming two night victories, was replaced as *Kommodore* of SG 4 by Oberst Druschel due to the poor performance of the *Geschwader* during operations over the Ardennes. The following day, the energetic Druschel visited III./SG 4 and instructed Leutnant Klepke to scout potential airfields in the area north of Wittlich and to the west of Cochem, which would be nearer to the front. But, as the *Gruppe*'s war diary noted;

'The *Geschwader* should transfer by *Gruppen* to airfields closer to the front in order to be able to fly shorter missions. The *Kommandeuren* are opposed to this plan, since shortening the flight reporting window would expose the taking off, assembling and landing of formations to even greater surprise attacks from the enemy than is already the case.'

But whatever disagreement over operational policy may have riven the commanders of SG 4, firstly they would have to see in the new year by flying – and surviving – an imminent, dangerous and radical new mission.

CHAPTER EIGHT

THE WEST AND EAST – 1945

While groundcrew brush snow away, pilots of I./SG 2 gather for a discussion in front of a pair of Fw 190F-8s of the *Gruppe* parked on a snow-packed taxiway in Hungary in January 1945. This may possibly have been at Csór, a landing ground 13 km west of Székesfehérvár. The aircraft in the foreground carries SC 50 bombs under its wings, and a pair of SC 250 weapons lie in the snow to the right foreground (*EN Archive*)

In late 1944, Generalmajor Dietrich Peltz, commander of II. *Jagdkorps*, decided that the best way in which to offer support to the German armoured thrust in the Ardennes was to neutralise Allied tactical air power where it was at its most vulnerable – on the ground. By using the element of surprise, Peltz concluded that as an alternative to costly dogfights against numerically superior enemy fighter formations, such an attack would incur minimum casualties and consume less fuel.

Originally intended to coincide with the launch of *Wacht am Rhein*, the weather had frustrated the plan. The operation, codenamed *Bodenplatte* ('Baseplate') was deferred, despite the commencement of the ground offensive. However, at the first suitable break in the weather (dawn on 1 January 1945), after highly secret preparations, German fighters from 33 *Gruppen* left their forward bases and flew in tight formation at low-level to attack several Allied airfields. Although surprise was achieved and moderate success gained at some targets, at others the results were nothing short of catastrophic. SG 4 also took part in *Bodenplatte*, and, unfortunately, it was in the latter category that the *Gruppe*'s operations can best be described.

Despite the fact that SG 4 numbered more than 150 Fw 190F-8s by this time for its 129 pilots, only around 55–60 machines were operational by 1 January, dispersed across several airfields. As happened on the airfields of all the units slated to take part in *Bodenplatte*, at Köln-Wahn, Major Weyert briefed the Staff and *Staffelkapitäne* of III. *Gruppe* during the afternoon of 31 December.

Weyert explained that a Ju 88 nightfighter acting as a pathfinder would guide the *Geschwader* across the heavily fought-for area of the Hürtgen Forest towards the target – the airfield at St Trond in Belgium, a former Luftwaffe nightfighter base and, by the time of *Bodenplatte*, home to a pair of P-47 Thunderbolt fighter groups of the USAAF's Ninth Air Force. The time of the attack was scheduled for 0925 hrs the following morning, and in addition to machine gun and cannon, the Fw 190s were also to carry *Panzerblitz* rockets.

The pilots of SG 4 were placed on alert at 0630 hrs on a bitterly cold New Year's morning, and the plan was for the three *Gruppen* to assemble into a *Geschwader*-sized force, with *Stab*, I. and III. *Gruppen* rendezvousing north of Bonn and then meeting II./SG 4 at a point five kilometres west-northwest of Zülpich. The plan did not work.

After a delayed take-off in sub-zero conditions, just ten Fw 190s of III./SG 4 headed towards the assembly point near Bonn, and as they did so they almost collided with another large Luftwaffe formation flying northwest. This was the Bf 109 and Fw 190 force of JG 11 making for its target of Asch airfield, northeast of St Trond. To avoid collision, Major Weyert quickly nosed downwards into thick ground haze, losing contact with half of his pilots in the process. Those remaining with him (the others had joined the JG 11 formation) pressed on for the next assembly point at Zülpich.

Just east of Zülpich, Weyert spotted around 25 Fw 190F-8s circling. Three of them then turned east, back towards German airspace, trailed by the other Fw 190s. Weyert assumed that the first three machines were those of the *Kommodore*, Oberst Druschel, and the *Geschwaderstab* and further assumed, therefore, that the mission had been cancelled. He tried to make radio contact with ground control for verification but was unable to. At 0920 hrs, Weyert turned with the other pilots of III./SG 4 and followed.

In fact, this had been a catalogue of misinterpretation, wrong assumption and error. The three aircraft Weyert had seen turning east were probably those of the *Stabsschwarm* of II./SG 4 under Hauptmann Hans Stollnberger. The only aircraft of SG 4 which continued westwards on the mission to St Trond were those of Oberst Druschel, and his wingman, and the five pilots of III./SG 4 who had joined the JG 11 formation.

As if SG 4's failure to reach St Trond was not bad enough, the *Geschwader* – and the entire *Schlacht* arm – would suffer a severe blow in the loss that day of the recently appointed *Kommodore*, Oberst Druschel. Inconclusion shrouds the circumstances of his death on 1 January 1945, but it is quite possible he was a victim of the American AA units active in the Hürtgen area at the time. Druschel was a stalwart

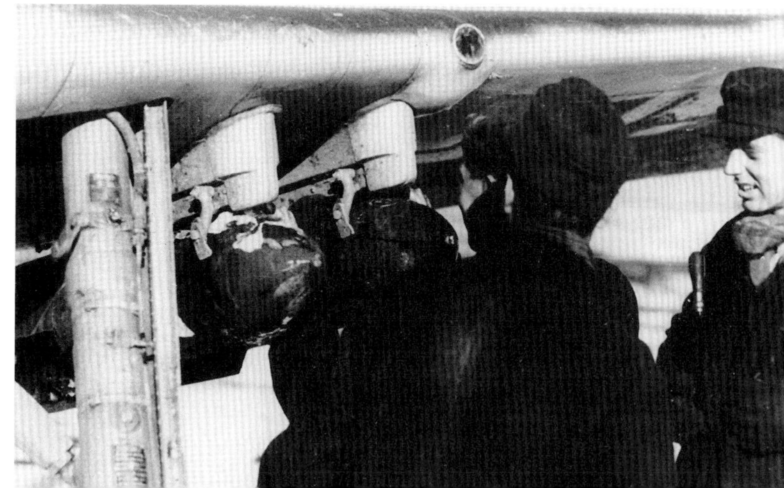

Armourers check the fitment of a pair of SC 50 bombs beneath the port wing of an Fw 190. Note the frost-covered aperture in the wing leading edge for a BSK 16 camera (*EN Archive*)

As the war entered its final year, so the toll in the number of experienced unit commanders rose. One such casualty was Major Theodor Nordmann, *Kommandeur* of II./SG 3. A Stuka veteran of the convoy battles over the English Channel, the Mediterranean and Crete, and later against Soviet armour in the USSR, he was awarded the Swords to the Knight's Cross on 17 September 1944 following the completion of 1140 missions. Nordmann was killed on 19 January 1945 when his Fw 190 collided with his wingman's aircraft in bad weather over East Prussia. By then he had flown 200 missions in the Focke-Wulf, including his 1111th flight, which saw him receive with a wreath and a plaque upon his return to base (*Robert Forsyth Collection*)

of the *Schlachtflieger*, serving as *Kommodore* of Schl.G. 1 and Inspector of Day Ground-Attack for the *General der Schlachtflieger*. A recipient of the Oak Leaves and Swords to the Knight's Cross, he was posthumously promoted to Oberst, having flown between 800–1000 combat missions.

Recent research indicates that altogether, nearly 300 Allied aircraft were destroyed as a result of *Bodenplatte*, of which some 145 were single-engined fighters. A further 180 aircraft were damaged and 185 personnel killed or wounded. *Bodenplatte* was, without doubt, an unexpected and painful blow for the Allies, but its effect on tactical operations would be negligible and, in the case of SG 4's intended target, virtually non-existent.

In total, 143 German pilots were killed or reported missing, including three *Geschwaderkommodore*, five *Gruppenkommandeure* and 14 *Staffelkapitäne*, with a further 21 pilots wounded and 70 taken prisoner. SG 4's known losses included Feldwebel Richard Heinz of 7. *Staffel*, who was shot down by Allied AA near Aachen, and Oberfeldwebel Hans Schmieder of 8. *Staffel*, whose Fw 190 was also hit by AA fire. He bailed out over Allied territory. Feldwebel Rudolf Fye of 9./SG 4 was shot down by P-47s, his Fw 190F-8 crashing near the road between Asch and Mechelen. It was equipped with *Panzerblitz* rockets, at least five live examples of which were discovered at the crash site, presenting Allied air and technical intelligence with a significant find.

But SG 4 did go on to make some impact. A week after *Bodenplatte*, on 7 January, 13 of III./SG 4's Fw 190s attacked American forces in the forests north of Bastogne. I. and II. *Gruppen* could not to take part in the operation because their airfields had been bombed. III. *Gruppe* returned without loss, but its pilots were unable to observe the effect of their attack. In the period 21 January–20 February 1945, the Fw 190F-8/9 of III. *Gruppe* accounted for the destruction of 23 Allied tanks, inflicted serious damage on 11 more and caused the destruction of two armoured vehicles. This tally was achieved over 115 sorties flown in 16 operational missions in which the *Panzerblitz* was deployed.

Other units continued to attack with bombs – the Fw 190s of Hauptmann Alexander Gläser's II./SG 77 were based at Naglowice, in southern Poland, in January 1945. The logbook of one of the *Gruppe*'s pilots, Unteroffizier Wilhelm Beyerlein, demonstrates how, in the six days from 13–19 January 1945, he logged one mission, on the 13th, as 'Bombs on tanks in woods' near Motkowice, and another mission less than two hours later as 'Bombs on tanks at Sobkow in 0133/4 – Good bomb strikes'. A third mission was broken off. On the 17th, in a mission flying from Schlosswalden, he noted 'Bombs on road east of Tschenstochau'. The next day, 'Bombs on tanks west of Tschenstochau'. Then, on 19 January, 'Bombs on Wielun. Hit by Flak. Good bomb strikes'.

By February 1945, a total of 115 *Panzerblitz*-equipped Fw 190F-8/Pb 1 aircraft were available, with 43,580 missiles having been manufactured in Czechoslovakia under the supervision of the SS. A monthly production rate of 16,000 missiles was targeted. Tactical doctrine for *Panzerblitz* deployment eventually settled on the fitment of eight rockets per wing, which were fired in salvos of four or in pairs.

An instructional memo issued by the OKL Operations Staff on 15 March 1945 describes the tactical deployment of the Fw 190 fitted with *Panzerschreck* and *Panzerblitz* rockets, but in reality, it describes the environment on the Eastern Front rather than the West, where the war against armour and railways was paramount;

'Apart from operations by Ju 87 *Panzerjägerstaffeln* with 3.7 and 7.5 cm guns, Fw 190 *Staffeln* equipped with "*Panzerschreck*" and "*Panzerblitz*" have proved increasingly successful in anti-tank operations.

'Attacks using Fw 190s so equipped are carried out against railway gradients of about 20 degrees and simultaneous firing of aircraft [on board] armament. The launch range for this type of attack is about 200 m. Because of the flatness of the trajectory, it is possible only to attack with or against the wind – side-wind attacks reduce accuracy of fire considerably. For tactical execution of these attacks, combined operations with ordinary Fw 190 *Schlachtstaffeln* have proved expedient in neutralising ground defences during attacks. In less defended areas, "*Panzerschreck*" and "*Panzerblitz*" *Staffeln* always carry an extra bomb under the fuselage.

'In the absence of heavy ground defence, tanks which have broken through, armoured vehicles and locomotives are promising targets for this type of Fw 190 *Staffel*. Attacks on tank concentrations (assembly points) and other *Flak*-protected targets are not feasible because of the necessity of an undisturbed and accurate approach flight and the short launch range.'

After the war, Hitschhold raised this while under interrogation by the Allies;

'The missions against tank assembly areas were a great mistake because these were always protected with many AA guns and resulted in high losses compared to completely unimportant accomplishments. For attacks on tank assembly areas it was better to use formations which carried a great number of containers of four-kilogramme hollow-charge armour-piercing bombs which could be dropped from halfway outside the effective AA fire zone.'

On 1 March 1945, following a devastating 50-minute artillery barrage combined with strikes directed at German positions by ground-attack aircraft, the Soviet 1st Belorussian Front launched an advance north towards Kolberg and the Baltic coast. The Germans were caught in disarray, panic broke out in the rear and roads in the area became congested with refugees streaming west. Amidst the collapse of his defence in the northern sector of the Eastern Front, Hitler was convinced that his senior and regional military commanders had failed him.

The *Schlachtflieger* were committed as fully as possible in holding back the Soviet thrust. The Luftwaffe had wanted to equip three specially trained anti-tank *Staffeln* with rocket-firing Fw 190s in

Austrian pilot Artur Pipan, seen here as a Hauptmann, flew his first combat missions in early 1941 in a Ju 87 of 5./StG 1 when he attacked Malta from Sicily. From 1 April 1943, he was *Staffelkapitän* of 5. *Staffel*, which was renamed 5./SG 1 in October 1943. Pipan became *Geschwaderadjutant* of SG 1 in April 1944, and he was awarded the Knight's Cross on the 6th of that month. Appointed *Kommandeur* of I. *Gruppe* on 1 March 1945, he had completed more than 750 operational missions – including 85 flown in the Fw 190 – by war's end (*Robert Forsyth Collection*)

each *Schlachtgeschwader*, but by mid-April 1945 only 3 and 6./SG 1, 9./SG 2, 6./SG 3, 7., 8. and 9./SG 4, 1., 3. and 13.(Pz.)/SG 9, 9./SG 77 and 13./SG 151 were equipped with the *Panzerblitz I*. In the case of Hs 129-equipped 13.(Pz.)/SG 9, having left Poland at the end of January, the *Staffel* went to Perleberg, northwest of Berlin, to begin conversion onto the Fw 190, but by 21 April 1945 it had moved to Wels, in northern Austria, where the unit reported having all 19 of its Fw 190s serviceable on the 26th.

In October 1945 Hitschhold wrote that, 'The delayed development of rocket projectiles was a great disadvantage. The combatting of certain targets like tanks and ships could have been considerably more effective. The goal of having every ground-attack unit equipped, if necessary, for anti-tank work with rockets was not attained. This was due to a delay in the early development. For the required training, no adequate amount of fuel could made available.

'Furthermore, the specialisation of anti-tank ground-attack units resulted in the disadvantage that because of their special training, they could only be used under certain circumstances and against tanks. Thereby, great breaks in operations often came about for such units in which they could not be used as ordinary ground-attack units. In general, the development in the field of rocket projectiles and the necessary sights began too late. The *Schlachtflieger* showed a way to combat targets effectively from low altitude and great ranges without coming into the anti-aircraft fire around the target.

'The lack of rockets, bombs or containers which gave good results in low-level attacks manifested itself especially in Russian offensives which were often conducted in bad weather. At such times, ground-attack aircraft had to be used mainly for strafing attacks because bombs dropped with delayed-action fuses had little effect.'

One example of such a scenario was that of III./SG 4 when it transferred from Köln-Wahn to Woisselsdorf, near Grottkau in Silesia, for operations in the East. When the *Gruppe* arrived there on 19 January 1945, it found the airfield had not been prepared for *Schlacht* operations, lacking ground equipment and with neither bombs nor *Panzerblitz* available.

Meanwhile, on 7 March, 16 Fw 190s of I./SG 1 attacked the bridge over the Oder at Zellin in the Kienitz bridgehead. They scored some hits but failed to destroy the bridge. To the south, three Fw 190s (one loaded with *Panzerblitz*) of the *Geschwader Stabsstaffel* of SG 3 under Major Bernhard Hamester operated against Soviet tanks of the 1st Ukrainian Front, claiming seven destroyed, three by rockets. Also in the air in the same area were Fw 190s of SG 1, II./SG 3 and 13./SG 151, which mounted 55 sorties against tanks.

In the process, the *Schlachtflieger* clashed with enemy aircraft, and they claimed two Yak-3s and one Yak-9 shot down, two of which were credited to Oberfeldwebel Helmut Mischke of III./SG 1 for his 43rd and 44th victories. Mischke was in the air again on 9 March, and was credited with no fewer than nine enemy aircraft, four of which were shot down while his Fw 190 still had its bombs attached.

In 1945 the need for Fw 190 *Schlachtflieger* to be proficient in aerial combat as well as ground-attack techniques was greater than ever. Oberfeldwebel Karl Stein flew with II./SG 1 under Major Ernst-Christian Reusch in early January 1945, and he recalled flying the Focke-Wulf on the Oder Front. 'We were very pleased with the Fw 190. It was very friendly to the pilot'. When it came to Soviet aircraft and pilots at that time, Stein remembered;

'Our thought was that they had beautiful aeroplanes, but they did not know how to fly them. They just made one pass – if they attacked us at all – and were gone. They always fired from much too far away and were hopeless at deflection shooting. They could climb much faster than us, whereas we could out-dive them. They could also out-turn us. Almost always they would just throw on power and pull back on the stick.

'There was one encounter when two of their fighters were on the tail of an Fw 190. I slipped in between the two of them and fired on the leader. He turned and I followed. Then he did a stupid thing, something you never do in a dogfight – he reversed direction. I missed him, but he turned again, and I got him. His wingman never fired at me – perhaps he was afraid of hitting his leader.

'But our infantry suffered heavily from Il-2 attacks, so we were anxious to get at them. I apparently got the rear gunner of one because his gun pointed upwards and I expended all my ammunition – guns and cannon – on that aircraft. He started smoking, his right landing gear dropped and he slowed way down. But I couldn't knock him down. When I broke off, he was still in the air, although he probably didn't make it back to base.'

Soviet forces broke out of the Görlitz bridgehead on 22 March, heading north, cutting Küstrin off. Advancing respectively from the Kienitz and Lebus bridgeheads, the 8th Guards Army and 5th Shock Army struck across the Küstrin corridor and united around Golzow. That day, SG 4, whose *Gruppen* had returned to the East, sortied 77 Fw 190s and accounted for some of the 17 enemy tanks and 15 vehicles destroyed. But it seemed that for every small 'win' there would be a significant loss. On the 26th, the Austrian *Staffelkapitän* of 3./SG 1, Hauptmann Hans Schalanda, an old 'Africa hand' who had flown 933 missions as both a dive-bomber pilot and a *Schlachtflieger*, was killed when his *Panzerblitz*-armed Fw 190 was hit by AA fire southwest of Küstrin. Schalanda had been awarded the Oak Leaves to the Knight's Cross on 24 October 1944.

Küstrin was in Soviet hands by midnight on 29 March. With the capture of the town, the Red Army now held a bridgehead about 50 km wide and seven to ten kilometres deep and was in a position to begin preparations for

Schlachtflieger of 1./SG 2 in typical late-war flying gear gather for a photograph in front of one of the unit's winter-camouflaged Fw 190F-8s in late 1944/early 1945. The only officer in the line-up is former Ju 87 pilot Leutnant Fritz Krey, fifth from left. At this time, 1./SG 2 was fighting in Hungary and retreating into Austria. Note the parachute placed at readiness on the Focke-Wulf's horizontal stabiliser. Krey survived the war, having flown 346 missions, including some with *Panzerblitz*-armed Fw 190s. He is credited with the destruction of three bridges, two tanks and several guns and vehicles (*Steenbeck*)

the final drive on Berlin, the first priority of which was to rebuild Küstrin's heavy-capacity bridges.

The *Gruppen* of SGs 1 and 77 were busy attacking the Göritz bridge on 8 April. Eight Focke-Wulfs from II. and III./SG 1 damaged it in three places, while II./SG 77 sent 30 Fw 190s to strike at Soviet motor transport moving between Breslau and Liegnitz, claiming 25–30 vehicles destroyed. The same units attacked a similar target in the same location on the 10th, blowing up a fuel tanker and destroying 40 vehicles. But again there were losses to the ferocious Soviet AA guns, including that of Hauptmann Anton Andorfer, another Knight's Cross-holder and the *Staffelkapitän* of 2./SG 77. He had flown around 200 missions in the Fw 190.

As the 1st Belorussian and 1st Ukrainian Fronts drove on to the Oder supported by large formations of ground-attack aircraft and SU-152 assault guns bearing formidable 152 mm weapons, wherever possible the Luftwaffe still attempted to provide fighter cover for the *Schlachtgruppen* as they fought to shield Berlin from the Soviet onslaught. On 16 April, for example, Bf 109s of III./JG 3 provided escort for Fw 190s of SG 3 attacking enemy formations west of the capital, while a *Schwarm* of Fw 190s from I./JG 6 gave cover to Focke-Wulfs of SG 77 when they bombed targets in the Bähren area. In addition to their escort role, the fighters of JG 6 carried AB 500 bomb containers, dropping them on targets en route to meet the *Schlachtflieger*.

To the southeast, over Czech territory, SG 4 was very active. On the 16th, in the Hodonin–Brno area, 46 Fw 190s of I. *Gruppe* strafed and bombed enemy positions and transport around Cejc, destroying 22 vehicles and an AA position and causing two explosions within a motorised column.

South of Raciborz, I. and III./SG 4, under Hauptmann Fritz Schröter and Major Hans-Edgar Weber, respectively, used *Panzerblitz* rockets in 76 sorties against infantry, artillery positions and vehicles around Köberwitz. As well as causing fires, *Panzerblitz* accounted for 12 tanks destroyed, another damaged and three artillery positions eliminated. However, the pilots of five *Panzerblitz*-equipped aircraft experienced technical problems with their rockets and some returned without firing a shot. North of Zgorzelec, II./SG 4 sent 38 Fw 190s to strafe and bomb enemy concentrations, inflicting some damage.

Equally, however, SG 4 was enduring considerable attrition. In the three days between 15–17 April, the *Geschwader* either lost or suffered damage to 22 of its Fw 190s, all, with one exception, F-8s. On the 16th alone, four were shot down by enemy fighters either over Hustopece or north of Opava, while two others were hit by AA fire and crashed in flames south of Opava and Annhof, respectively. The missing included Oberleutnant Willi Osterburg of 2./SG 4, a former ferry pilot, and Feldwebel Karl Zieske of 7./SG 4, who was shot down by AA fire southeast of Opava.

To the west, in the Triebel area on the 16th, I. and III./SG 77 under Hauptmann Hans-Joachim Brand and Hauptmann Gerhard Stüdemann, respectively, deployed no fewer than 60 Fw 190s, along with four Ju 87s of 10.(Pz.)/SG 77, to attack Soviet positions and tanks. Pilots reported that enemy artillery positions and vehicle assemblies were struck more than 60 times during the attacks, and fires were seen burning. However, due to heavy clouds of smoke and dust caused by the attacks, detailed assessment of the results was not possible.

Stüdemann, *Kommandeur* of III. *Gruppe*, wore the Oak Leaves to the Knight's Cross. He would fly 173 missions in the Fw 190 and had an impressive record as a 'tank-killer'.

This Fw 190F-8/R1 of III./SG 77 was found abandoned in woods at Pardubitz (Pardubice) in east Bohemia at war's end. By this time the *Gruppe* was under the command of Hauptmann Gerhard Stüdemann. Lying on the ground to the left is what appears to be an AB 250 drop container used to hold SD 1, SD 2 or SD 10 *Splitterbomben*, while to the right, next to the open crate, are a pair of wooden practice containers (*JaPo*)

As a measure of the intensity of operations despite unreliable supplies of fuel, parts and ammunition, as well as regular attacks on their airfields, the Fw 190s of II./SG 4, III./SG 77 and *Stab* and II./SG 2 flew 182 sorties on 17 April in the area of *Luftflotte* 6. To the south, the Fw 190s of Hauptmann Karl Kennel's I./SG 2 arrived at Graz after staging through Bohemia.

17 April also saw 1./SG 2 carry out a final mission against enemy AA units near Fürstenfeld. Upon their return to Graz, the Fw 190s were pushed back into well-camouflaged dispersals at the edge of a forest. There was no longer any fuel. The *Schlachtflieger* waited until American forces approached the airfield, at which point they blew up their Focke-Wulfs with hand grenades.

On the 18th, I./SG 77 absorbed another blow when the Fw 190 of its *Kommandeur*, the highly experienced combat veteran, Hauptmann Hans-Joachim Brand, was downed by light AA fire while attacking Soviet armour near Alteno airfield, five kilometres east of Luckau in Brandenburg. The Knight's Cross-holder was a Stuka veteran of the Polish and Western campaigns and had taken part in the convoy battles in the English Channel in 1940. By the time of his death, Brand had flown 964 missions, including around 150 in the Fw 190. He had been nominated for the Oak Leaves.

It seems OKL had begun to recognise the hopeless predicament of allowing attrition to steadily eliminate its *Schlachtgruppen* in the East, and on 19 April orders were issued to move I./SG 77 south to Niemes-Ost/Höflitz, rather than into the territory of the recently formed *Luftwaffenkommando Nordost* in northern Germany as originally intended. The *Gruppe* would be followed south to Pardubitz, in Bohemia, by *Stab* and III./SG 77. Meanwhile, I./SG 77 went to nearby Niemes-Süd/Kummer, where it joined *Gefechtsverband Rudel* alongside the *Stab* and II./SG 2, the Ju 87G '*Kanonen-Vogel*' ('cannon birds' fitted with 37 mm underwing cannon) of 10.(Pz.)/SG 2 and the Fw 190D-9 fighters of II./JG 6, all under the command of famed Stuka ace Oberst Hans-Ulrich Rudel, at this time *Kommodore* of SG 2.

But by late April it had become ever-more dangerous for the *Schlachtflieger* to be in the air. Markedly symbolic of how crushing Allied air power had become were the events of the morning of the 30th when Fw 190Fs of I.(Pz.)/SG 9 returned to Sülte-Banzkow, an emergency landing ground close to the cover of some woods south of the Schweriner See, having carried out a rocket attack against Allied armour and vehicles. I.(Pz.)/SG 9 had been established in January 1945 with its 1., 2. and 3. *Staffeln* formed by redesignating 12.(Pz.)/SG 9, 10.(Pz.)/SG 1 and 10.(Pz.)/SG 3, respectively. 1. *Staffel* had converted from the Hs 129 to *Panzerblitz* Fw 190s in November 1944, 2. *Staffel* retained the Ju 87G until the capitulation and 3. *Staffel* exchanged it Stukas for *Panzerblitz* Fw 190s in March.

Just as the Focke-Wulfs made their approach, pilots of No 350 (Belgian) Sqn, which happened to be patrolling the Schweriner See area at 8000 ft in their Spitfire XIVs, spotted them. Leading the three aircraft of the unit's Red Section was Plt Off Desmond Watkins, and they dropped down to attack out of the sun. The next few minutes

Fw 190F-8 'Yellow K' of Oberstleutnant Georg Jakob's SG 10 lies abandoned in the grass at České Budějovice in southern Bohemia. This was one of several aircraft from the unit found at České Budějovice at the end of the war, by which stage the *Geschwader* had been tactically subordinated to *Luftflottenkommando* 4 (*JaPo*)

would result in a heavy blow for the *Schlachtflieger* and the loss of three Knight's Cross-holders.

As Watkins described in his subsequent combat report, he and his wingman closed behind three of the Fw 190s and then opened fire. One 'rolled over and crashed into flames' and another 'cartwheeled and broke up on the strip'. A few moments later, Watson engaged a third Focke-Wulf, firing a long burst from dead astern. This machine 'wallowed badly and crashed into the wood by the strip in flames'. The Spitfire pilots claimed three Fw 190s destroyed and another damaged in their attack.

Gruppenkommandeur Hauptmann Andreas Kuffner had been leading the formation, which also included Oberleutnant Rainer Nossek, *Staffelführer* of 3.(Pz.)/SG 9, and another *Staffelführer*, Oberleutnant Wilhelm Bromen. All three men were seasoned Ju 87 pilots, and Kuffner had received the Oak Leaves on 20 December 1944 in recognition of 60 enemy tanks destroyed. Together, they had flown some 2500 missions. Nossek was credited with the destruction of 73 tanks and Bromen, who had flown around 300 missions in the Fw 190, had 76 tanks to his name.

Perhaps it was Generalmajor Hitschhold who, in a post-war report for the Allied victors, summarised it best;

'The prerequisite for successful and lasting ground-attack operations is air superiority. Wherever the Germans did not have air superiority, their ground-attack operations were almost ineffective. This lesson was confirmed in Africa, in Italy and on the Western Front. There, suffering from high losses of aircraft, planned and effective support of ground-attack operations was *not* achieved. A raising of the number of ground-attack units would only have been useful if air superiority could have been won back.'

APPENDICES

COLOUR PLATES COMMENTARY

1

Fw 190A-5/U3 Wk-Nr 1123 'Red L' of Leutnant Armin Rohnstock, 6./Sch.G 1, Deblin-Irena, Poland, spring 1943

Finished in an RLM 74/75/76 mottle, with the 74 prevalent along the dorsal edge of the fuselage, although the engine cowling is finished in a dominant 75, almost giving the appearance of a different assembly. The aircraft has the *Gruppe*'s Mickey Mouse emblem in a red circle applied to the cowling and yellow (RLM 04) theatre fuselage band, wingtips and cowling underside. These yellow markings were usually applied at the point of manufacture. The early black triangle marking of the *Schlachtflieger* has also been added aft of the *Balkenkreuz*. The spinner was tipped in the *Staffel* colour.

2

Fw 190A-5/U3 'White M' possibly of 5./Sch.G 1, probably Ukraine, March–April 1943

Finished in typical mid-war camouflage of RLM 74/75/76 on fuselage and uppersurfaces, with a rear fuselage theatre identification band, underside wingtips and lower cowling in yellow for the Eastern Front. The aircraft is fitted with both centreline and underwing bomb racks.

3

Fw 190A-5/U3 'White B' + 'Bar' of 5./Sch.G 2, Sicily, late summer 1943

Finished in RLM 74/75/76, with heavy application of 74 and 75 along the cowling and fuselage dorsal surfaces, and a tail assembly and rudder more mottled. The aircraft has a white Mediterranean theatre fuselage band and underwing tips. The *Gruppe* horizontal bar and propeller spinner are tipped in the *Staffel* colour. The *Geschwader* used large white letters for codes.

4

Fw 190A-6 'Black Chevron and T' + 'Bar' of Hauptmann Johannes Meinicke, *Staffelkapitän*, 1./Sch.G 1, Bryansk or Konotop, USSR, August–September 1943

When appointed as commander of 1. *Staffel*, Meinicke retained the 'T' on his aircraft, which he had carried when *Gruppe* Technical Officer of I./Sch.G 1. The other fuselage markings denote a *Stab* aircraft, although the horizontal bar tended to signify operations rather than technical. The yellow theatre fuselage band has been almost obscured by RLM 71 or 80 green.

5

Fw 190A-5 Wk-Nr 1112 'White B' of 1./SG 152, Deblin-Irena, Poland, late 1943–early 1944

Most likely an aircraft passed to training unit SG 152 from another operational *Gruppe*, 'White B' carries typical ground-attack markings, with the aircraft code and the black *Schlacht* triangle (retained for the unit's training machines) having been applied over earlier markings. The yellow band denotes an aircraft operating in the East and the unit's emblem is a plainer variation of the Mickey Mouse insignia associated with the *Schlachtflieger*.

6

Fw 190A-5 'Black L' of an unidentified *Schlachtgeschwader*, Eastern Front, winter 1943–44

Finished for winter operations in a light coating of white, which has begun to wear with the passing of time and exposure to weather, as well as being stained by the engine exhaust. The spinner is probably black and white, and the areas of yellow (RLM 04) remain visible on the underside of the cowling, wingtip undersides, the base of the rudder and, unusually, around the fuselage and *Balkenkreuz*.

7

Fw 190F-3 'White I' + 'Bar' of 4./SG 3, East Prussia, winter 1943–44

Possibly an A-6 converted into an F-3, this Fw 190 is finished in a common mid-war scheme probably comprising RLM 74/75 on dorsal edges and fuselage, with RLM 04 yellow theatre markings. The spinner tip in white is for 4. *Staffel*.

8

Fw 190F-8 'White 1' possibly flown by Oberleutnant Heinrich-Hans Karras of 1./SG 4, Viterbo or Rieti, Italy, spring 1944

The aircraft's standard European camouflage has been oversprayed in overall RLM 79 sand yellow and then mottled in RLM 80 green. The spinner features a black and while spiral. The white Mediterranean fuselage recognition band and *Balkenkreuz* national marking are partially covered by the RLM 79 and the tail *Hakenkreuz* is almost masked. The *Gruppe* emblem depicts Mickey Mouse astride a bomb wielding an axe.

9

Fw 190F-8 'Yellow 0' + 'Yellow I' of 9./SG 4, Laval or Avord, France, June 1944

Little photographic evidence exists of III./SG 4's Fw 190s in the West in mid-1944, but this aircraft was captured on film at Avord carrying a yellow code along with a vertical bar, possibly denoting a *Staffel* adjutant or technical officer. It is possible the rudder was also yellow.

10

Fw 190F-8 'QS+AB' of Hauptmann Fritz Schröter, *Gruppenkommandeur*, I./SG 5, Pontsalemjoki or Salmijärvi, Finland, summer 1944

As *Gruppenkommandeur*, Schröter had his aircraft marked with the somewhat unusual code letters QS+AB. The 'QS' appears to have been applied over an earlier yellow fuselage band, which was itself covered by a darker colour, possibly RLM 75. The letter 'A' was probably in green to denote a *Stab* aircraft, and it was also applied to the mainwheel door cover. Yellow RLM 04 was also to be found beneath the engine cowling and lower rudder, but not under the wingtips. The fitment of a 300-litre drop tank suggests a long-range ferry flight had been made. Underwing racks were absent.

11

Fw 190F-3 'White L' + 'Bar' of 4./SG 1 (East Prussia) or 4./SG 2 (Poland and Rumania), summer 1944

This aircraft is mostly finished in a dense application of RLM 74/75/76, with RLM 75 having been applied in areas that have seen overpainting of previous codes. Cowl assembly has a markedly different finish to the rest of the machine, with RLM 76 clearly visible against a wavy demarcation line of RLM 75. A white II. *Gruppe* bar overlays the yellow theatre fuselage band.

12

Fw 190F-8 'White F' of II./SG 77, possibly Seifersdorf, Poland, summer 1944

Finished in layers and mottles of RLM 74/75/76, this aircraft, probably of the *Gruppenstab*, carries the horizontal *Gruppe* bars either side of the mid-war *Balkenkreuz*, as was the practice of II./SG 77 at this time. Application of letters to individual aircraft, however, has been retained, and in this case the letter 'F' is visible on the engine cowling. The underside of the latter is probably in yellow.

13

Fw 190A-4 'BK+WV' and 'White 24' of 1./SG 101, Reims, France, February 1943–April 1944, or Wischau, Czechoslovakia, April 1944–February 1945

Built by Focke-Wulf at Bremen or Marienburg, and within the 627–652 *Werknummer* production batch, this A-4 would probably have been passed on to training unit SG 101 following service with another operational *Gruppe*. The red fuselage band indicates this may have been a fighter unit. The *Staffel*'s Fw 190s and Bf 109s carried large white numbers on their cowlings to enable easy identification in the air by instructors and trainee pilots, and for assembly and formation practice.

14

Fw 190F-8 of I./SG 10, Udetfeld, Germany, December 1944

Probably a factory-fresh aircraft assigned for testing purposes, it appears to have been finished in a base of RLM 75/76, but with sporadic mottles of a green, possibly RLM 73, applied. *Balkenkreuz* is of the later style, and the cowling ring and rudder are in yellow. The Fw 190 is fitted with an ETC 501 centreline rack and underwing EG-Pb racks for *Panzerblitz* rockets.

15

Fw 190F-8/R1 'Chevron/Red 2' of II./SG 2, Börgönd or Szőc, Hungary, January 1945

In the winter of 1944–45, several, if not all, the aircraft of II./SG 2 received various styles of winter camouflage, some more 'elaborate' than others. This Fw 190 is finished in RLM 74/75/76 and oversprayed in a white scribble, with the exception of the engine cowling ring which appears to be darker, in RLM 72. The single chevron, possibly denoting a *Gruppe* Adjutant, is well defined, but the tactical number '2' less so, with the edges softened by the winter white. The yellow RLM 04 fuselage band is also partly obscured. The black and white spiral spinner, introduced by *Luftflotte* 4 from 20 September 1944, has been crudely finished. Wing undersides also have the yellow 'V' recognition markings, likewise introduced by the *Luftflotte*.

16

Fw 190F-8 'Black 9' of II./SG 2, Börgönd or Szőc, Hungary, January 1945

Finished in a style similar to 'Chevron/Red 2', 'Black 9' features a more prevalent white scribble. While its yellow fuselage band remains visible, it appears no yellow underwing 'V' recognition markings were applied. The aircraft's mainwheel doors have been removed and there is an unusual closed-up double white line on the spinner.

17

Fw 190F-8/R1 Wk-Nr 588717 'Chevron'/Green 3' + 'Bar' of *Stab* II./SG 2, Milovice, Protectorate of Bohemia and Moravia, early 1945

This Fw 190, with its chevron and horizontal bar, may have been the aircraft of the *Gruppe* Operations Officer, but it also retained its individual tactical number '3' in green as a *Stab* machine. The spinner has a bold black and white finish in conformity with *Luftflotte* orders. *Balkenkreuz* is of a later style, lacking black outlines, but the tail *Hakenkreuz* is of a muted black outline form only. The darker finish of the fuselage extends only to the tail assembly join, this latter structure being of a much lighter finish of a sparse mottle, possibly RLM 75/76. At some point, the aircraft's wheel well doors were removed.

18

Fw 190F-8 'Chevron/Yellow K' of SG 10, Ceské Budejovice, Protectorate of Bohemia and Moravia, April 1945

The aircraft appears to have been finished in a dark splinter pattern, probably either RLM 70/71 or 71/72. From its yellow code letter, it is possibly an aircraft of 3. *Staffel*, but used by the *Gruppe* Adjutant. The *Balkenkreuz* is of late-war style. The entire tail assembly may have been a replacement section, being finished in a highly contrasting mottle of RLM 74/75/76.

19

Fw 190F-8/R1 'Black 3' + 'Bar' of *Geschwaderstab*/SG 10, Ceské Budejovice, Protectorate of Bohemia and Moravia, April 1945

Similar in colour to 'Chevron/Yellow K', 'Black 3' featured an RLM 70/71 pattern, although it was much more random and not in the harder-edged style of a splinter pattern. It has an unusually small late-war *Balkenkreuz* and a short chevron forward of it, together with a horizontal bar aft, indicative of a *Geschwader* Operations Officer. The presence of a numeral code as opposed to a letter, however, is puzzling. The aircraft appears to have had a coloured cowling ring and rudder, both possibly yellow.

20

Fw 190F-8/R1 'Black 6' + 'Bar' and 'White 70' of *Geschwaderstab*/SG 10, Ceské Budejovice, Protectorate of Bohemia and Moravia, April 1945

'Black 6' shows the same code style as 'Black 3', being another *Stab* machine, but there the similarity ends. It is finished in the later RLM 80/81/82, with dorsal edges giving way to a mottle on fuselage sides and tail. The aircraft may have previously served with an operational training unit, hence the large number '70' on the cowling, before being taken on by SG 10. It also has a yellow cowling ring and white-striped black spinner.

BIBLIOGRAPHY

In addition to German and Allied documents and reports, the following published sources were consulted:

Articles

Arthy, Dr Andrew, 'Last Days of the Cannon Birds – Luftwaffe Junkers Ju 87G anti-tank operations, Eastern Front, April–May 1945', *The Aviation Historian* Issue 37, October 2021

Corum, James S, 'The Luftwaffe's Army Support Doctrine, 1918–1941', *The Journal of Military History* Vol 59, No 1, January 1995

Corum, James S, 'To Stop Them on the Beaches – Luftwaffe Operations against the Allied Landings in Italy', *RAF Air Power Review* Vol 7, No 2, Summer 2004

Dill, Arno, 'Focke Wulf sur la Tunisie, 1 & 2e partie', *Air Fan* Nos 100 and 101, March and April 1987
Musciano, Walter A, 'They Flew for Franco: German Condor Legion's Tactical Air Power', *Aviation History*, 2004
Naylor, Edwin W, 'The Life of Oberst Dr. Ernst Kupfer – The Bamberger Horseman', *Air War Publications*, 2017
Stenman, Kari, 'The Short Saga of Battle Unit Kuhlmey', *Air Enthusiast* No 34, September–December 1987

Books

Anttonen, Ossi, *Luftwaffe in Finland/Suomessa 1941–1944, Vol 2*, Helsinki, 1980
Arthy, Andrew and Jessen, Morten, *Focke-Wulf Fw 190 in North Africa*, Classic Publications, 2004
Arthy, Andrew and Jessen, Morten, *Focke-Wulf Fw 190 in the Battle for Sicily*, Air War Publications, 2010
Bergström, Christer and Mikhailov, Andrey, *Black Cross Red Star – The Air War over the Eastern Front Volume 2: Resurgence January-June 1942*, Pacifica Military History, 2001
Bergström, Christer, *Kursk – The Air Battle: July 1943*, Ian Allan Publishing, 2007
Bergström, Christer, *Bagration to Berlin – The Final Air Battles in the East: 1944–1945*, Ian Allan Publishing, 2008
Brütting, Georg, *Das waren die deutschen Stuka-Asse, 1939–45*, Motorbuch Verlag, 1984
Buchner, Hermann, *Stormbird – Flying through fire as a Luftwaffe ground attack pilot and Me 262 ace*, Hikoki Publications, 2000
Cooling, Benjamin Franklin, (Ed.), *Air Support*, Office of Air Force History, United States Air Force, 1990
Corum, James S, *The Luftwaffe – Creating the Operational Air War, 1918–1940*, University Press of Kansas, 1997
Farkas, Jaroslav, Janda, Ales and Poruba, Tomáš, *Focke-Wulf Fw 190s of Jagdgeschwader 6 in WWII Final Operations*, JaPo Publishing, 2024
Fleischer, Wolfgang, *German Air-Dropped Weapons to 1945*, Midland Publishing, 2004
Frappé, Jean-Bernard, *La Luftwaffe face au débarquement allie 6 juin au 31 août 1944*, Editions Heimdal, 1999
Hazard, Marc, *La Stukageschwader 2 "Immelmann" Tome II: Septembre 1943–Mai 1945*, Editions LELA Presse, 2020
Hermann, *Dietmar, Focke-Wulf Fw 190 F und G vom schnellen Jäger zum Jagdbomber und Schlachtflugzeug – Entwicklung, Produktion und Einsatz*, Stedinger Verlag, 2012
Imrie, Alex, *Pictorial History of the German Army Air Service 1914–1918*, Ian Allan, 1971
Janda, Ing. Aleš, and Poruba, Ing. Tomáš, *Focke-Wulf Fw 190 F, G*, JaPo, undated
Manrho, John and Pütz, Ron, *Bodenplatte: The Luftwaffe's Last Hope – The Attack on Allied Airfields, New Year's Day 1945*, Hikoki Publications, 2004
Nauroth, Holger, *Stukageschwader 2 Immelmann*, Verlag K. W. Schütz, 1988
Obermaier, Ernst, *Die Ritterkreuzträger der Luftwaffe 1939–1945, Band II Stuka- und Schlachtflieger*, Verlag Dieter Hoffmann, 1976
Pegg, Martin, *Hs 129 Panzerjäger*, Chandos Publications, 2019
Plocher, Generalleutnant Hermann: *The German Air Force versus Russia, 1943*, USAF Historical Division, Aerospace Studies Institute, Air University, Arno Press, 1967
Proctor, Raymond L, *Hitler's Luftwaffe in the Spanish Civil War*, Greenwood Press, 1983
Rajlich, Jiri, Kokoska, Stanislav and Janda, Ales, *Luftwaffe over Czech Territory 1945*, JaPo, 2002
Shores, Christopher and Massimello, Giovanni, with Guest, Russell, Olynyk, Frank and Bock, Winfried, *A History of the Mediterranean Air War 1940–1945, Volume Three, Tunisia and the End in Africa*, Grub Street, 2016
Smith, J Richard and Creek, Eddie J, *Focke-Wulf Fw 190 Volumes Two 1943–1944 and Three 1944–1945*, Classic Publications, 2012 and 2013
Spenser, Jay P, *Focke-Wulf Fw 190 – Workhorse of the Luftwaffe*, Smithsonian Institution Press, 1987
Weal, John, *Osprey Aviation Elite Units 13 – Luftwaffe Schlachtgruppen*, Osprey Publishing, 2003
de Zeng IV, Henry L, and Stankey, Douglas G, *Dive-Bomber and Ground-Attack Units of the Luftwaffe 1933–1945 – A Reference Source, Volumes 1 and 2*, Midland Publishing, 2009 and 2013

Websites

www.ghostbombers.com by Nick Beale
www.ww2.dk *The Luftwaffe, 1933–1945* by Michael Holm, including *Luftwaffe Officer Career Summaries* by Henry L deZeng IV and Douglas G Stankey

INDEX

Page numbers in **bold** refer to illustrations.
Some caption locators are in brackets.